Accountability...A Noun or a Verb?

To order additional copies, please contact us.
BookSurge, LLC
www.booksurge.com
1-866-308-6235
orders@booksurge.com

Accountability...A Noun or a Verb?

Richard L. Cassidy

2006

Accountability...A Noun or a Verb?

TABLE OF CONTENTS

Special Thanks   ix

Guilt Admission   xi

Chapter One   Introduction   I

Chapter Two   Accountability – The Noun   15

Chapter Three   Accountability – The Verb   23

Chapter Four   Take The Risk   33

Chapter Five   Accountability Anonymous Prayer   47

Chapter Six   Can't Be A Victim   59

Chapter Seven   Need A Vision   73

Chapter Eight   Belief In Self   87

Chapter Nine   You Are Not Alone   IOI

Chapter Ten -   You Are Only Accountable For You   II3

Chapter Eleven   Ending At The Beginning   II7

SPECIAL THANKS

To Ann, Dan, Geri, Liz, and Scott, a sincere thank you for investing your time and insights into the completion of this book.

To Betsy, although I had to stay on you to complete your review of this book, thank you for your constant love and inspiration. You motivate me to be accountable and work harder and harder every day to be a better lover and friend.

GUILT ADMISSION

Throughout the book, I will misuse two words. Every dictionary I checked defined the word "accountability" as a noun. I will constantly be referring to it as a verb to reflect the need to take action to truly demonstrate accountability. I also misuse the word "better" as a noun to serve as a generalized reference to anything in life that you want to improve. I refer to this as the betterment that we are all aiming for in life. Obviously, it is up to you to define this "better" for your own life.

CHAPTER ONE

Introduction

More than anything else I can think of, having a victim mentality will keep you from succeeding. It will suck the life right out of your will to improve. It will create the false belief that you have no say in the outcomes in your life. Remember, success should not be tied directly to outcomes but to how you respond to the circumstances you face in life. Your behaviors and your responses are all that you can control and, thus, are the true measure of your character and success in life.

I have often been accused of stating things in an extreme fashion, sort of stretching the facts somewhat. I am married to a CPA who often whips out the GAAP rules to correct my exaggerations. I know she means well and she will probably correct the statement I am about to make, but I will make it anyway. (Of course, I can only hope I survive revealing this about her!)

I firmly believe that ALL humans have a strong desire to be successful at the things they do in life. This desire for success is tied to the innate human need to be happy and fulfilled. Whatever we do, we want to be successful. Regardless of how complacent we may seem to act, deep down we all desire things that will improve the likelihood of our success. Now, some of us are better than others at translating this desire into action. It is one thing to want to lose weight; it is an altogether different thing to actually follow through with this desire and cut back on the number of trips through the buffet line. Action orientation is not often one of our strengths. We are all better suited to "talk the talk" versus "walking the walk."

> If you haven't the strength to impose your own terms upon life, you must accept the terms it offers you.
> – T.S. Eliot

All of us are also different, with diverse values, interests, skills, and desires. We all have different motivators that we seek to stimulate every day. Regardless of differences, I believe we share a common desire to get better at whatever we want to be. Unfortunately, many of us fall short of following through on this desire. Few of us ever reach the upper limits of our potential, much less go beyond them. This is one of those things we can never prove, but, if true, makes you wonder why. Why is there so much untapped potential in this world?

I am reminded of a quote from the former great Green Bay Packer coach Vince Lombardi who said,

> "I firmly believe that any man's finest hour, the greatest fulfillment of all that he holds dear, is the moment when he has worked his heart out in a good cause and lies exhausted on the field of battle victorious."

How many of us ever truly "lie exhausted?" We may think we are exhausted, but have we ever truly "worked our hearts out?" Have we given our hopes and dreams our very best shot?

These are tough questions we must ask ourselves as we journey toward "better" every day of our lives. Consider the answer to this question right now: If you have not been exhausted, does it bother you deep down in your inner soul? Do you feel like you are selling yourself short?

Many of us manage to convince ourselves that we have worked our hearts out when in reality we have not. Instead, we seek the quick fix (the fad diet, the inspirational book, the latest craze seminar), anything that can become the means to a greater end. None of these things are bad and can even lead to meaningful gains. I enjoy reading the works of people like Tony Robbins as much as anyone. *Seven Habits of Highly Effective People* by Stephen Covey is probably the greatest book I have ever read and I make it a point to read it every year (this past year was my 10th reading). I applaud those who turn the desire to improve into action and seek out these resources. Unfortunately, I believe we view these resources as the end all, placing complete faith in these resources as some sort of magic bullet that will correct all of our ills. We all desire the "fix" but do not want to go through the necessary journey toward improvement. We do not want to truly be "exhausted on the field of battle."

Many of us simply do not know, or choose to ignore, the important first step that we must take BEFORE seeking the latest fad diet or reading an inspirational book if we want to create meaningful and sustaining change. This first step is critical in order for us to truly make personal change for the better. This "better" takes many forms in our everyday lives - a better friend, a better baseball player, a better pet owner, a better spouse, a better engineer, a better runner.

In order to be better at anything, we must accept that we are in control. Each of us is accountable for where we have been, where we are, and where we are headed. Whether you like it or not, you are accountable for where you are in your career, the type of relationship you have with your children, your physical health, and your general state of being. Being "better" is not about placing faith in the latest diet or inspirational book; it is about placing faith in self and believing that you can create this better place in your life. Being accountable for self is at the center of having faith in self.

> "Life moves on, whether we act as cowards or heroes. Life has no other discipline to impose, if we would realize it, than to accept life unquestioningly. Everything we shut our eyes to, everything we run away from, everything we deny, denigrate or despise, serves to defeat us in the end. What seems nasty, painful, or evil, can become a source of beauty, joy, and strength, if faced with an open mind. Every moment is a golden one for him who has the vision to recognize it as such."
> --- Henry Miller

Obviously, there are some things we cannot control. If you have had the unfortunate experience of contracting cancer or diabetes, for example, you probably did not have any say in this. However, you have full say in how you respond to it for the rest of your life. I have read about the many special heroes in this world who did not allow just terrible circumstances to dictate how they responded to life. These people had no regrets about being stricken with cancer or some other terminal illness. Instead, these heroes have maintained control of their lives and not only reached the upper limits of their potential but actually strove to expand those limits. They lay "exhausted" every day of their lives and their battlefields were much tougher than most of ours! We could all learn valuable lessons from them.

If you happen to be a college basketball fan, one of the best players in the country this year is Adam Morrison from Gonzaga University. By the time you read this, he will likely be playing in the NBA. If you get a chance, watch him play. During timeouts, watch what he does; he is checking his blood sugar level and taking insulin shots. He is a type I diabetic playing in a league of some of the greatest athletes in the world. He is accountable and has set no limits for himself. He is a hero!

One of the most inspirational things I have ever read was in *Seven Habits* by Stephen Covey, in which he tells the story of Viktor Frankl and his experiences in one of Germany's notorious Nazi death camps. One can only imagine not only the physical abuse the prisoners received, but the mental and emotional anguish as well. Despair, hopelessness, and despondency are just some of the images that come to mind.

Frankl decided that although the situation seemed to allow him no control over the outcome, he would nonetheless be in control. Regardless of what the Germans did to him and although it seemed as though his every freedom had been taken away from him, there was one freedom that remained his and only his and he determined to exercise this freedom to the fullest every day while in the death camp. Frankl discovered that we are all granted a small space between every stimulus we ever experience and the response that we provide. This space belongs to each and every one of us and only to us. No one can ever take it away. It is a true human right…an entitlement. And, in reality, it is your responsibility. To quote Frankl:

> "Ultimately, man should not ask what the meaning of his life is, but rather must recognize that it is he who is asked. In a word, each man is questioned by life; and he can only answer to life by answering for his own life; to life he can only respond by being responsible."

That is powerful! In the worst of circumstances, Frankl said, "no, you cannot take this tiny space away from me. You cannot control how I respond to what you are doing to me. I am *still* responsible!" Frankl demonstrated that even under the most stressful moments in life, we can still seek comfort in knowing that we still have control. Regardless of circumstances, we control our destinies!

Think about how many times in life you let things that seemed quite mundane compared to Frankl's circumstances control how you live, thinking yourself the victim of some negative force "out there" that is out to get you. How often do you catch yourself saying or feeling "Woe is me!" Now, imagine if we all responded as Frankl did. Would you be a more successful person? Would you be reaching the upper limits of your potential? Would the world be a better place?

Every day is filled with these stimuli that trigger responses and, whether you realize it or not, you are using these tiny spaces that are owned exclusively by you to make decisions or take actions that determine where you have been, where you are today, and where you are going in the future. Thus, whether you like it or not, you are accountable by virtue of owning this space. Even when you choose to take no action, you have still made a choice within that tiny space.

In this space, you decide if you are going to go for that new job. You decide if you are going to cut back on the sweets or whether or not to get out of bed to go for that run on a cold, rainy morning. You decide if you are going to be critical of your child or use the opportunity as a teaching moment to help him/her understand the mistake made. You decide if you are going to wait and study at the last minute or prepare fully for final exams. You decide if you are going to surprise your spouse with a special gift for no rational reason whatsoever. You decide if you are going to be in competition with the other person whom you just want to "beat" or to be in competition with yourself to become the best you can be regardless of what the other person does. You decide if you just want a passing grade or to go for the very best grade you could achieve. You decide if you are merely a victim of certain stimuli or someone who views the situation as an opportunity to learn and grow.

> "If a man is called to be a street sweeper, he should sweep streets even as Michelangelo painted, or Beethoven composed music, or Shakespeare composed poetry. He should sweep streets so well that all the hosts of heaven and earth will pause to say, 'Here lived a great street sweeper who did his job well.'" - Martin Luther King, Jr.

This space defines our effectiveness, which I believe is key to our success. (Someone once told me that being effective in life is more important than being right. And this is so true! No matter how "right" I might be, I will not be able to get anything out of this "rightness" if I am not effective with it.) In this space, we decide our response to the stimulus, and this response is always some type of behavior. Our behaviors determine our effectiveness, which drives our success.

I do not think anyone would argue that individually we are in complete control of our behaviors. Thus, if you believe the above statements, we each control our success. It all starts with accepting the accountability for the space that exists between the stimulus and your response. In reality, there is no accepting required since you own the space regardless of your choice.

The story of Viktor Frankl is one of three inspirations I have in writing this book, but by far the most powerful. I remember the first time I read it and needing to read it again and again and again. It hit home with me so strongly, making me realize that I do have the freedom to choose. I can make a difference in my own life and where I am headed. I can be the best (fill in the blank) that I care to be regardless of what any "force out there" tries to do.

Obviously, there are some "physical" limits to this. I cannot will myself to be a better golfer than Tiger Woods. I could never work really hard over the next six months and expect to beat Michael Jordan in a slam-dunk context. Some skills are natural and part of this journey is all about understanding our unique skills and desires. I do, however, firmly believe that we each have a special "destiny" inside. The tough part is figuring out where that special place is...that special place where our skills and desires meet in a beautiful and synergistic union.

My second inspiration is a sincere desire to see people succeed. This is reflective of the coach inside of me. Growing up, I thought I wanted to be a football coach. My false paradigm was that coaching only took place in sports. During my first real job was as a career counselor for college athletes, I quickly realized that coaching takes place in many diverse walks of life and that I was actually a coach whose underlying motivation was to "coach" others to succeed. I have been very fortunate to replicate this type of coaching role in different settings as a counselor, consultant, change manager, or facilitator. No matter the role, the underlying inspiration has remained the same. I want to help people individually and collectively succeed at whatever the circumstance calls for.

The final inspiration, which is the latest one that really pushed me over the top to write this book, is the growing trend in personal behavior observed in the world around us. Too many of us are "victims." We feel entitled to things and if we do not get them, we blame every possible thing around us instead of looking within to ask why our "misfortune" happened or what we could have done differently.

I am reminded of the hit song from the 1980's by Michael Jackson that has a chorus that states:

> "I'm looking at the man in the mirror. I'm asking if he'll make a change. And no message could have been any clearer. If you want to make the world a better place, take a look at yourself, and make a change."

Needless to say, being accountable and making personal change is extremely difficult! We are all well-suited and very comfortable passing a critical eye over the other guy, but not turning the same eye on ourselves. It requires more vulnerability and humility than we average humans typically possess. It takes a very special person to be able to always look first at self whenever things go bad. We are much better at placing blame.

For instance, in all the companies I have worked for in my career, I have always had a leadership team that I facilitated. Typically, these teams were composed of some pretty smart and successful individuals, usually vice-president level types or what is referred to as "top management." It has always amazed me how often these people would blame "them" for all the challenges that occurred. Whenever anything negative happened, "they" did it to us. "They" needed to communicate better, etc. Rarely was the mirror held up to say "what can WE do differently?" A victim mentality was all too often a part of the norms of behavior. Obviously, this is not healthy and does not reflect a spirit of accepting accountability.

The opposite of this is something I have often observed in people with physical handicaps. For some reason, despite being dealt a bad hand, people with handicaps seem to overcome their limitations to live life to the fullest. They never seem to complain or act like victims although society would say they are. And yet, those of us with no real handicaps say "Woe is me" all of the time. Imagine what it would be like if you were struck with blindness, say, to never again see a beautiful sunset on the beach, the snow falling from the sky, or the smiling face of a child? How would you respond?

It is my wish that we all take full accountability for the space between stimulus and response, which we already own. It is my desire that we all firmly believe that in doing so, we can make changes in our lives that will lead to greater success. Each one of us is accountable and empowered for defining what success should look like. It is my wish that we all carry a little mirror in our back pockets to use whenever we start to place blame on others or feel like victims. When these situations arise, each of us should quickly take a look in the mirror and ask "what could I have done differently?"

Please note that this is not about being perfect or measuring up to society's expectations. This is all about taking accountability for our own effectiveness and giving life our very best shot. Once we accept this accountability, quick fix solutions become secondary. For example, accepting accountability for our health is exponentially more powerful than doing the latest fad diet. At the end of the day, if we truly accept this accountability, we will have a long term commitment to better health and this destiny will be achieved. We will explore every possible avenue toward better health by virtue of saying "I am accountable for my health." We will lie on our "health" battlefields exhausted and victorious.

Our story begins by defining accountability and what it means to accept accountability. As you learn about the things you must do to put your accountability into successful practice, keep in mind that there are no height or weight requirements involved. No special degrees or "pedigrees" needed. No discrimination based on sex, race, or national origin. It is a basic human right to own this space between stimulus and response. In this space, you decide your responses and behaviors. These behaviors then define your effectiveness, and your effectiveness determines your success. It is my hope that you are willing to accept this and begin your journey toward a greater destination in all of the roles you play within your own life. I hope that you want "better." Obviously, it is your right to not want "better" but I am willing to make another one of my extreme comments and say that by virtue of reading these words right now you indeed do want "better." Congratulations! You have taken the first step toward accepting your human right of accountability for personal success.

One more thing to keep in mind: This is not a mountain to climb where a clear ending will be within sight. It is a never-ending journey of personal exploration, learning, development, and rediscovery…a never-ending cycle of growth. This is both good and bad. The bad is that we all desire endings. This gives us a sense of closure and accomplishment. Unfortunately, if you are truly committed to yourself, there will be no ending. The good is that there will be plenty of milestones along the way to celebrate small victories. And it will be critical to your long-term commitment (and sanity!) to celebrate these to ensure you rejuvenate regularly.

Furthermore, this is not the easy road. It is much easier to be a victim, taking zero accountability for your destiny. It is much easier to place blame on others or on circumstances. It is so much more difficult, but rewarding, to say "I'm in charge here! I may have been knocked down, but I am still on my journey toward success. I am going to figure out where I went wrong, what I could have done differently, and come back even stronger than before as I continue my journey toward greatness." There is greatness inside of each of us. It is our job to find it and be personally accountable for maximizing it.

Meanwhile, we must always remember that we have every right to seek fulfillment in all that we do, never settling for contentment and never being a victim! Good luck! I hope this book helps you on your journey. Life is not supposed to be lived with a mentality of "just getting by." It is meant to be lived to the fullest, to truly "live" life, taking it all in, and wanting more. I firmly believe we all want to live life this way. Something may have come along and knocked us down. But, we all have every right to get back up, take control, and start reaching the fullest potential inside of ourselves.

Rules For Being Human

You will receive a body. You may like it or hate it, but it's yours to keep for the entire period.

You will learn lessons. You are enrolled in a full-time, informal school called life.

There are no mistakes, only lessons. Growth is a process of trial, error and experimentation.

The "failed" experiments are as much a part of the process as the experiments that ultimately "work."

Lessons are repeated until they are learned. A lesson will be presented to you in various forms until you have learned it. When you have learned it, you can go on to the next lesson.

Learning lessons does not end. There is no part of life that doesn't contain its lessons. If you're alive, there are still lessons to be learned.

"There" is no better than "here." When your "there" has become "here", you will simply obtain another "there" that will again look better than "here."

Other people are merely mirrors of you. You can not love or hate something about another person unless it reflects to you something you love or hate about yourself.

What you make of your life is up to you. You have all the tools and resources you need. What you do with them is up to you.

The choice is yours.
-Dr. Cherie Carter-Scott

CHAPTER TWO

Accountability – The Noun

"You must take personal responsibility. You cannot change the circumstances, the seasons, or the wind, but you can change yourself. That is something you have charge of." –Jim Rohn

Accountability is defined as a state of being answerable. It is a state of being able to act without superior authority. In other words, the buck stops where accountability resides. If you are accountable, you are in charge. You do not need to seek permission. However, you also cannot blame others if things go wrong. As stated, the buck stops with you and you are in control. In reality, although we do not like this, we cannot fall victim to anything related to us if we are truly accountable.

Individually, we all have certain accountabilities whether we like it or not. If you forgot to do your homework, the ole "dog ate my homework" trick will not work. The teacher will still hold you accountable. I remember a guy I played high school football with who was notorious for jumping off-sides. He would literally get called for this penalty three or four times every game. When we studied the game film, our coach would get so mad with him, but he would swear up and down that he did not do it. He would always say that the referee blew the call.

Now, obviously, the game film did not lie. It showed each time that he clearly jumped off-sides. Yet, my teammate would never accept accountability. He was just a victim of a blind referee. Too bad the camera would not lie!

We are all accountable for simple things such as abiding by laws, getting to work on time, paying our bills, and not cheating Uncle Sam on our taxes. We have the final say on how we spend our money, who we choose as friends, how many trips we take through the buffet line, and where we send our kids to school.

Given that I am a simple-minded person, let's take an even narrower view of this. I believe that the only thing we are really accountable for in life is our behavior. That's it. Now, you may say that on your job, you are accountable for a certain monthly report. Well, I would still say that what you are really accountable for are the behaviors you exercise to deliver the best on-time report possible. You may say that you are accountable for managing a multi-million dollar project, but once again I would say that what you are really accountable for are the behaviors that will deliver the project on time and on budget. I think you can always bring your accountability back to behavior.

Our behaviors say everything about who we are. They are our walk. (Our walk is composed of the decisions we make and the actions we take throughout the course of every day of our lives. I will refer to our walk later in the book as a comparison to another part of who we are: our talk.)

Our behaviors are the things we do all day long. In reality, our behaviors are really all we are. They define our character and our personality, forming the fabric of everything that everybody sees in us. They reflect our values and everything that is important to us whether we realize it or not. Most importantly, they are the one absolute thing that we can control within our individual lives.

I remember when I was in high school at a student government conference and motivational guru Dan Clark was giving the keynote address. He said something that is obvious, but so powerful and lasting. He said that he could care less if you talk the talk. Walking the walk is what determines success. He repeated over and over again, "if you are going to talk the talk, you must walk the walk!" The walk is what matters. The walk displays our character and personality and determines our success.

> "The world is moving so fast these days that the man who says it can't be done is generally interrupted by someone doing it."
> - Elbert Hubbard

The walk is the actions you take every day of your life and these actions are your behaviors. You may think that you are defined by a degree, a family name, looks, or some other "physical" trait or material possession. I would argue that at the foundation of who you are today and will become in the future are your behaviors. They reflect what's important to you, your values, your motivators, your desires. They define your character. Although society places a high value on things such as degrees, looks, and pedigrees, it is ultimately your character that determines your TRUE success and fulfillment in life.

As mentioned earlier, we each have this space that occurs between stimuli and our responses. We own this space as it is a human entitlement. And we have no choice, it is ours and we are in complete control of it. It is in this space that every single solitary behavior we ever have takes place. No behavior ever occurs without a stimulus. In this way, we are always reactionary. We own these behaviors (you can call them actions if you'd like; I just like to think of them as behavior, reflective of character, integrity, and being).

So, when I think of "accountability the noun", I think of behaviors. If you asked me today what I am accountable for, I would say that I am accountable for how I respond to life. I cannot control life, but I completely control how I respond to it. And, regardless of how bad I may look in the mirror sometimes, I am accountable for every one of my behaviors. (On the flip side, I fully blame a greater being for how I physically look in the mirror. No one can hold me accountable for being short and a little "stumpy!" Lucky for me, my wife has bad eyesight.)

Now, being sensitive to those who have impairments such as severe neurological disorders, I completely understand that there are people with real disabilities that prevent them from controlling their behavior. These are real disabilities and society should show compassion for these people. However, for most of us and most likely all who are reading these words, our heads work just fine. In turn, there is no escaping the accountability you own for your behaviors. You spend every day deciding how you are going to respond to life's never-ending stimuli. Twenty-four/seven is spent assessing stimuli, deciding how to respond, and then behaving. All of this happens almost subconsciously.

If accountability is simply synonymous with the word behavior, then once again, we are accountable. There is no escaping the fact that you do not need superior authority to approve your daily behaviors. Now, there are circumstances where we should listen to superior authority before acting (such as the police before going 80 mph in a 55 zone). But at the end of the day, we are still in complete control in deciding how fast we are going to drive. We decide every behavior we ever take in life. (Even when impaired such as when you have had too much to drink, you have chosen your behaviors. You may not know the behaviors you choose after your 10th drink, but you were completely in charge when you decided to have drink no. 1, and then no. 2, and so forth. Again, this makes you in charge and accountable.)

This is the great thing about being human. Other species have instincts that cause them to respond to stimuli in certain (and mostly predictable) ways. This is a little bit boring when you think about it. As humans, however, we have freedom of choice. We get to decide how we respond to life. We decide if we are aiming for contentment or fulfillment every day that we live.

Every day is filled with stimuli and, realizing it or not, we respond to them with our behaviors. These responses take place after that little space where we decide how to respond. We each own this space; it is ours to keep forever. I know I sound like a broken record, but it is the most important point to take away from this book. This space is where you build your dreams, your better health, your better friendships, your better financial situation, your better parenting skills, and your better career. You respond to these dreams with behaviors. These behaviors either move you backward, keep you stationary, or take you on the journey toward the destination you truly desire.

It is completely up to you. You are accountable. Your behaviors are totally within your control. The ones you chose every day in response to life's stimuli determine your effectiveness and ultimately your success. Sleeping in and skipping that morning run is a behavior. Never letting a day go by that you do not exercise for at least 30 minutes is a behavior. Investing that extra time preparing for a mid-term exam is a behavior. Planning for retirement today even though you are only 30 years old is a behavior. Blaming the government for not giving you a more comfortable retirement through social security is a behavior. Deciding that you are too tired to spend some time playing with your kids when you get home from a long day at work is a behavior. Taking the time to let your spouse vent about her day, just so she can get it out of her system, is a behavior.

I think you get the picture. Our effectiveness in life is the sum total of all of the individual behaviors that we choose every single day. The choices are up to you. Sure, we are all granted mulligans (in golf, the "do-overs" or "gimmes"). I am a die-hard weight lifter and runner. But when I eat out, I am going to choose the most chocolate-drenched dessert on the menu. This is one of my mulligans. But, just as in golf, we are not allowed to take a mulligan on every hole. Ultimately, by doing so, we are cheating. In life, the more mulligans we choose to take, the more we are just cheating ourselves. With accountability, there are no "gimmes."

So, when we look at accountability as a noun, there is no decision to be made. Whether you like it or not, you are accountable by default for your behaviors. The buck stops with you on every behavior you ever have.

This view of accountability is a default setting for each of us in life. It is a given. Unfortunately, this given does not produce results. This given does not make us strive to maximize our potential. This given does not push us to find that better we all seek in life. This given, as a noun, is stationary. As a noun, "lying exhausted on the field of battle" is not an image that comes to mind. To me, nouns are a little too stagnant.

The next chapter will take a different look at the word accountability. This look will allow you to decide whether or not you truly accept accountability. It is also a look that you may not like. It will require you to use that mirror to take a hard look at yourself. It will force you to make tough choices for the better you are aiming for in life. This look is not stationary, but all about taking action. It is all about walking the walk.

Responsibility
"Something I'm learning, something that I know is true.
The only person responsible for your actions is you.
What goes around, comes around, as you may have heard.
You give and take, you receive what you deserve.
As much as I may not want to admit,
this mess that I'm in, I got myself into it.
What I've done, I've done a couple of times.
They say you live and learn, well why didn't I?
So I'm dealing with the pain, and taking on the ache
I have to lie in the bed I didn't mean to make,
so instead of looking up 2 heaven and asking God 4 help

I'll take a look in the mirror, a good look at myself.
I have to realize and accept what I've done wrong,
learning lessons is tough but not if you are strong."
-Amber Rose

CHAPTER THREE

Accountability – The Verb

"I think there is something, more important than believing: Action! The world is full of dreamers, there
aren't enough who will move ahead and begin to take
concrete steps to actualize their vision." — W. Clem-
ent Stone

In every dictionary I have reviewed, accountability is always
defined as a noun. But to make this more interesting, I want you
to imagine what your world would be like if accountability was
instead a verb and you fully accepted it that way. Would things
be different? Let me explain.

When you think of a verb, action comes to mind. I have a
four-year-old son and some of the limited words he really un-
derstands are verbs like "run," "jump," "catch," "eat," "pee-pee,"
and, of course, "pooh-pooh." I think young children grasp these
words because they can see them happening. That's the essence
of verbs; they are actions you can see and feel. They are the
"walk." (I realize that "talk" is also a verb...but talking does
not really require action on your part. As the old cliché goes,
"talk is cheap.")

"If we wait to foil a bank robbery or rescue someone
tied on the railroad tracks we will never be a hero. We

probably won't even come across a cat stuck in a tree. As long as we sit at the bus stop waiting for our great moment we will miss our real chance at the heroic: the infinite number of tiny daily acts inspired by the great. Our actions may seem insignificant, but their results will grow and multiply." – Timberland Boots

As mentioned before, we are all inherently accountable for our behaviors. I said this was a human entitlement. Now, I am going to backtrack on this view. My real view is that we will not really accept accountability unless we treat the word as a verb. Unless it is action, it is not true accountability. So, as a noun, you are accountable by default. But as a verb, you have the freedom to choose if you are going to be truly accountable.

Let's look at some examples.

We all have financial responsibilities. One of these is preparing for our retirements. Now, I realize that we all have Social Security out there to help with our retirement. But I hope for your sake (especially if you are my age or younger) that you are not holding our government accountable for the financial security of your golden years. In reality, we are each accountable for our retirement nest egg. I view this accountability as a noun. It is a given, with no accepting necessary. You have this accountability by default.

If we look at this from the verb perspective, I would say that you are not truly accepting this accountability unless your behaviors today (your actions) reflect a true demonstration of this accountability. If you truly accept accountability for your retirement financial security, then you are taking action today to prepare for your golden years. I do not care if you are 25 or 55. If you are not trying to maximize your company's matching 40IK program, you are not truly accountable. If you do not have a firm understanding of your monthly free cash flow and translate that into a savings plan, you are not truly accountable. If you do not know what your projected retirement amount will be based on your current savings balance, you are not truly accountable.

Now, you may say that you do not understand these financial concepts. That is completely fair. However, we all understand retirement and the need for money. If you are truly accountable, you will turn your financial ignorance into a plan to seek knowledge. The Internet is full of knowledge. There are unlimited financial advisors out there ready, willing, and able to fill your knowledge gap. And, remember, choosing not to take action is just as much of a behavior (a choice you make) as seeking financial knowledge. It is just not a very safe one in this case.

Of course, there are some who say "live for today" and probably prepare very little for retirement. That is fair as people have the right to let this be their response. However, these people remain accountable for their financial situation upon retirement regardless. Unfortunately, this type of response to accountability (treating it as a noun) will not likely lead to financial security upon retirement. This may be your goal, but I doubt it.

Accountability is not the knowledge, it is the behavior. If you seek out help in planning your retirement, you are acting with accountability. You have taken action. No time is better than right now to truly take accountability (the verb) for your financial security by behaving appropriately. Take action right now to demonstrate this accountability. Make accountability a verb in your life!

If you are fortunate enough to have been blessed with a child of your own, you will know that as a parent, you are accountable for your children and their security, well-being, etc. As a noun, this accountability takes the simple forms of a warm bed, a roof over their heads, food, and other basic necessities.

From the verb perspective of accountability, parenting takes an entirely different form. I am reminded of another Covey statement from *Seven Habits* where he defines love as a verb instead of a noun. The same concept applies here. As a noun, love means "having a warm attachment or affection." As a verb, it means "to cherish, demonstrate passion and devotion for." Which version of love would you prefer to receive? I have a warm attachment to a lot of meaningless things in life (like Chinese buffets), but I cherish my son.

When my son was two years old, we noticed that he did not interact very well with other children on the playground at his daycare. Whenever I picked him up, I noticed that he would be off playing on his own. This led to an evaluation by an early childhood development group. All sorts of "scary" things came from this evaluation. Everything from sensory disorder to possibly autism ran through our minds.

As a parent, I had extreme and polar opposite reactions. On the one hand, I experienced denial. This was my son and nothing could possibly be wrong with him. He is just him and will develop in his own time, I told myself. On the other hand,

I wanted to crawl under a rock and just ignore what I was hearing.

In the end, accountability the verb paved the way. My wife and I listened to all who provided guidance and took action accordingly. We translated our accountability for our son's well-being into action. Our behaviors as parents led us to act accountably versus just being accountable (love as a verb and not just a noun).

We started two therapy sessions a week. One was for speech and the other for gross/fine motor skills (occupational therapy). At home, we took more active approaches (and thinking) regarding the types of toys we bought for him and the structure of his days. We wanted to do all that we could to stimulate his thinking and exercise those "skills" in which he was delayed. We did not want to just love him; we wanted our actions to show our love for him. This may seem like semantics, but there is a difference.

We started evening "exercise" time. Each evening before bed, we structured some time where we read books, worked on number/letter recognition and writing, did dramatic play, and even some "strength" exercises. (Before you begin questioning my parenting skills, these were basic exercises to strengthen his fingers for example, which are critical for writing skills. My wife would not let me start him this early on bench pressing and squats, although I wanted to!!!)

Accountability the noun may not have led to these actions. The noun is passive, which could have led to a response such as "there is nothing wrong with my son" or "he is just a little delayed," or "he will develop in his own time." Accountability the verb says that you are willing to do whatever it takes, then taking the action to make a difference. Accountability the verb says that no matter how I am feeling, I do not skip exercise time with our son.

What is ironic is how our son senses the love involved during exercise time, which we still do with him everyday. I truly think he appreciates the dedicated time we spend with him. (I vividly remember nights when I may have hinted to him about skipping exercises and he quickly corrected my ways. Without knowing it, he reminded me that accountability should be a verb.) Obviously, there are lots of "high fives" and positive reinforcement taking place during exercise time. The reinforcement I receive is how proud he is when he sees that I am proud of him. Love as a verb is so much more powerful than love as a noun! Actions will always be louder than words!

We know our actions with our son have made a difference. Now four years old, he has just "graduated" from speech therapy, having recently been assessed at six months ahead of his age. When I pick him up from daycare, I notice that he has become a "chip off the ole block" as a very social extravert. He is the one initiating play with others. He is the loud one. He is the one wanting to do group activities. He can recognize and write all letters, as well as numbers through 100. Obviously, I am enthusiastic and proud of all of this, but isn't this what parenting is all about?

If we had not treated accountability as a verb, where would my son be today? He may very well have been fine. He may very well have still developed normally at his own pace. But he could also have fallen further behind and developed additional developmental problems. This was not a risk I wanted to take as a parent. Your love for someone else should not be left to chance and I was definitely not going to leave my love for Rick to chance. I hope I will always treat my love for him as a verb.

Being passive (treating accountability as a noun) is to leave things to chance. Things that are truly important to you (like your children) should never be left to chance. Accountability as a verb is all about not leaving things to chance. It is about doing all that you possibly can to influence the outcomes you experience in life.

By treating accountability as a verb, we are not only talking, but walking. The walk is what will determine our success, our growth, and our future. We are all looking to make a difference in this world and to leave our mark and legacy. Legacies are made by verbs, not nouns.

Think about this in your own life. Think about the people you have admired, who you thought lived life the way it ought to be lived. Were these people talkers or walkers? I am willing to bet that they were walkers. They let their actions do their talking. These people treated accountability as a verb.

Larry Bird was one of the greatest basketball players to ever play the game. One of his best skills was free-throw shooting. Well, he did not become one of the NBA's greatest free-throw shooters by just saying, "I am accountable for my free-throw shooting." He achieved this by going out every day and taking action. He spent countless hours doing nothing but shooting free-throws. Think about how boring that would be, just standing there in the same spot and shooting a ball into a basket with no immediate reward except knowing that you are truly taking accountability for your success. You have turned this accountability into action and you will reap the benefit of your efforts. Larry Bird turned his accountability for the success of his free-throw shooting into a verb. He did not leave it to chance.

It is not about talking the talk, but walking the walk. Action drives results in life. If you are truly accountable, you treat accountability like a verb. You turn every accountability you have in life into a verb, an action, a response, a behavior. You choose behaviors that will drive your success. It means nothing to say you are accountable. It is all about turning this into actions that demonstrate that you are in charge.

All of this occurs in that space between stimulus and response. If you are truly accountable, you will choose a response (a verb, an action) that drives you toward greater success. This could relate to your career, financial security, relationships, health, or any other circumstance you experience in your life. This happens for each of us all day long, every day of our lives. You own these decisions. Obviously, the decisions taken will make all the difference in your level of success.

Be a walker! For every circumstance you face in life, define an action you can take to move toward your ultimate goal. When you start doing this, you are beginning to treat accountability as a verb. Now, by truly accepting accountability for you, I am willing to bet that you will move closer to maximizing your potential.

"A man is the sum of his actions, of what he has done, of what he can do, nothing else." - Mahatma Gandhi

CHAPTER FOUR

Take The Risk

Risk
There are no guarantees
Life throws things at you
You can catch or miss them
But they will come, ready or not

I always looked for the real thing
Never trusting in the possibility
Risk-taking not my forte
Staying safe at all costs

Even playing it safe is not certain
Safe has hurt me
Zero risk gets zero gain
Sometimes playing it safe costs you more

It has me,
In not fighting the battle
you may lose the war
In not believing in a dream
You may never sleep peacefully again

So let go of the fear
Reach out for the flame

So what if you get burned
Better that then numb for life

Better to remember passion and joy
Along with the pain and tears
Then to have no memories worth
Remembering

So to hell with safe
I am going to gamble and bet
Until I win back everything I lost
And my life is what it was meant to be
-   Michelle Mckee

Most of us are risk averse. We like things to be steady and predictable. And, of course, we like to do things that have a high likelihood of success. If given the choice, most of us would take the "for sure" average outcome versus the "risky" great outcome that also has the potential of being a bad outcome. There is nothing wrong with this behavior. It is just how many of us respond to life.

Part of this risk aversion is driven by societal pressures. The winners are usually the ones who receive the praise. They are the ones who win the trophies. The last time I checked, there was no trophy for the team that lost the Super Bowl. No one truly ever likes to lose and most of us downright hate it. Society places a higher value on those who win and, unfortunately, this often keeps many of us from competing when there is a chance of losing. We would rather avoid the risk than take a chance on winning. Some of us just choose not to be in the game. This is driven by that desire to avoid the so-called shame and disgrace of being a "loser." Now, obviously, all of this shame and disgrace is created within our own minds. Society has conditioned us all too well to respond this way.

> "One of the things that my parents taught me is never listen to other people's expectations. You should live your own life and live up to your own expectations, and those are the only things I really care about."
> - Tiger Woods

Another part of this risk aversion is the normal desire we all have to be content. And, far too often, we correlate this content with being happy. Once we get into a risky situation that could lead to failure, we know that we are also wagering our happiness. Even though the potential outcome might be greater happiness, most of us would rather not risk the happiness level we currently have. This is the natural human response and we choose once again to stay out of the game. How often do you see people become "couch potatoes" in life, with so much potential being wasted?

I believe that far too often we convince ourselves to set our happiness threshold way too low. I further believe that this tendency is driven by how easily we accept contentment in our lives. And although we may think we are content, I believe that if we accept contentment for too long, we actually become stagnant. Stagnation over time will actually cause regression and eat away at our current level of happiness. Thus, although we may think we are aiming to maintain our current level of happiness, we are likely to lose it by accepting contentment. Risk aversion behavior can actually be a risky proposition!

Unfortunately, better requires getting in the game and taking the risk. In order to get better, you have to be willing to give up wherever you are today. If you want a more challenging career, you have to be willing to give up the steady, yet boring job you currently have. If you want a more meaningful relationship, you have to be willing to let go of the stagnant one currently consuming your energies. If you want to lose weight, you have to give up the "comfort" (and great taste) of all those sweets you are consuming. If you want to become a better golfer, you are likely going to have to give up something else to invest more time on the practice greens. There are no shortcuts.

There are also no guarantees. You may end up with an even more boring job or a worse relationship. This is the price of aiming for better. The bottom line is that by taking action, there is the risk that you will not get the outcome you desire. That is the nature of the game and makes "take the risk" a key step toward truly accepting accountability for the better that you desire in life. If there was no risk, then, in reality, we would not really be humans with the capacity to think, learn, adapt, and grow. (And, of course, this would also make life way too predictable and boring!)

Accepting accountability takes tremendous courage, especially if you treat the word as a verb. It takes a willingness to openly admit the shortcomings, flaws, and limitations that we each have. It takes a willingness to say "hey, this is me; good, bad, or indifferent, this is who I am." It takes a willingness to risk failure. It takes vulnerability.

Vulnerability is one of my favorite words. It is all about having a capability for being wounded with no worry of being truly defeated. In most cases, especially in the context of what I am talking about, wounded does not relate to the physical but the mental and emotional states inside each of us. Vulnerability is a willingness to take a hit to our mental and emotional beings. It is all about being open to failure with no fear of repercussions, meaning no fear of the shame and disgrace that society sometimes places on failure. Unfortunately, mental and emotional wounds can sometimes hurt much more than physical ones and can last much longer. Our physical bodies are made to heal quickly when injured. Unfortunately, our hearts and minds do not always work this way when injured mentally or emotionally.

"When we were children, we used to think that when we were grown-up we would no longer be vulnerable. But to grow up is to accept vulnerability. To be alive is to be vulnerable." - Madeleine L'Engle

I remember the first date I had with my future (and current!) wife. I had had previous relationships, but nothing real serious. I had a feeling, though, the first time I met Betsy that she was really special. I obviously wanted to make a strong first impression and win her heart. (Ironically, our first date almost did not happen. My father had emergency open-heart surgery a few days before the date. We made a deal that if he was recovering well by the day before our date, the date would stand. As fate would have it, his recovery went well.)

A few months earlier, I had attended one of those all day motivational speaker seminars. This particular one had a long agenda of speakers, including Colin Powell and Zig Ziglar, just to name a few. One of the speakers was talking about personal success and kept reiterating the criticality of vulnerability to personal effectiveness. Vulnerability makes a leader seem real, which is vital to having people believe and follow the leader. It is a willingness to show flaws and say "hey, I am just like you; I am not perfect either!"

These principles of having a willingness to completely expose your inner being and also to say "this is me" with no regret really stuck with me. I remember recalling these principles in the hours leading up to this first date. I did not have a desire to "impress" Betsy. I just wanted to completely be myself. Obviously, as a short and stumpy person, this was risky considering that Betsy was absolutely stunning! The upside of the risk of course was the potential of starting a real and meaningful relationship with a wonderful human being.

So, we went to dinner and got back to her apartment around 10 p.m. The next thing I knew it was about 3 a.m. We had spent five hours sharing our inner most thoughts and feelings about every topic in the world. (I cannot recall a person in this world besides Betsy that I have spent a cumulative five hours talking to about anything, much less in one sitting. Of course, the one exception to this would be the topic of Clemson football with anyone willing to listen!) There were no "no-fly" zones, no hidden agendas, and no long pauses to make sure I said the "right thing."

I had spent five hours being completely vulnerable with another person. I had laid it on the line regarding my beliefs, values, and personality. Fortunate for me, there was a spark. Every day since then, we have explored how to love (as a verb) each other on a deeper level. And maintaining vulnerability has been a key aspect of the strength of our relationship. As a result, I truly believe we have as special a relationship as any happy couple. We are best friends and best lovers...true partners!

This all started through vulnerability. We had a willingness to share our flaws with no fear of repercussions. I took the risk of showing Betsy that "hey, this is me; we are either a fit for one another or we are not." I could have just tried to act like and say what I thought she wanted to hear. I could have tried to "impress" her. I could have left some things unsaid to protect myself from my flaws. I could have chosen not to show vulnerability and just faked it in order to attempt to look good.

And this may have worked. We may have spent the next 12 months or so in a less than real relationship. We may have even gotten married without knowing those vulnerable spots within one another. We may have had some regrets, but stuck it out for the next few years, although not completely satisfied, but content (and afraid of "losing"). We may have had a child and, for a few years, the child may have been the focal point of our love. But, as the child grew, there would still have been something missing and some type of wall starting to grow between us. Finally it would have come to a head and we would have begun to drift apart. Ultimately, the relationship would have ended in an ugly divorce with an innocent child torn in the middle.

Do you know any partners like this who spend years drifting apart (or operating in a state of numbness) simply because they are not vulnerable with one another? Do you know of any partners who are afraid to let their defenses down? For those who do, it is really a shame. Too many people are missing the magical experience of becoming "one" with another. This "oneness" is only achieved through vulnerability from both sides of the partnership.

Vulnerability does not just apply to relationships. You may have felt pressured to choose a particular career path because of family history. For example, every member of your family may have always gone into the family business and you felt this pressure as well. It was the easy choice and you knew you would be content with this choice. But, inside, that "better" was eating away at you. Well, you could either choose to let it eat away at you or you could show some vulnerability and say "hey, this is me and the family business does not fit."

This takes tremendous courage. But, at the end of the day, you are accountable for your happiness. And, as bad as this may sound, your happiness has to come before your family's in this situation. As the ole cliché states, you have to love yourself before you can love another. And your family's real goal should be your happiness, not your involvement in the business. If not, then I would question their motives. (Unfortunately, in way too many cases, things such as the family business end up tearing down the love of a family.)

Career change is one of the toughest areas to take risk, especially if you have family/financial obligations. You may be in a situation today that does not allow much risk taking. Financially, the steady paycheck is something you cannot afford to interrupt at this time. I would encourage you to not lose sight of your desired better. I would encourage you to devise a plan that will allow you to take the risk as soon as you can. It may not be tomorrow, or next week, or next year, but never lose sight of this desired better so that when the day comes, you are ready for action.

At the end of the day, if that better is nagging away at you inside but because of family or financial obligations you cannot act on it, it is also most likely impacting your ability to be an effective spouse or father or mother. It is tough to separate the emotions of one situation with the realities of another. Your spouse will know something is wrong, either by just knowing you or as a result of the way it is making you behave. In other words, everyone in your family is likely better off if you take the risk and act on your desire for better. Ironically, in this situation, although your aim may have been to protect your family, you may have actually been hurting them instead.

In all of these examples, you may be content with where you are. But life should not be lived for content. It should be lived for fulfilled! And there is a big difference between content and fulfilled. To "content" anything is to limit actions or requirements. This is directly counter to the way we have defined accountability. Accountability is to take action, to not set limits and to take the risk to achieve the better we all desire. We should all aim for "fulfilled," which can be defined as putting into effect and taking action to achieve the better we are seeking.

Being wounded is not something any of us actively seek in life. Whenever you take a risk, there is a probability for failure. This probability may be small or large, depending on the situation. Courage comes into play as you say that you do not care if you fail. You view not acting on the desire for better as the real failure. None of us like the pain that comes from being wounded. None of us wake up in the morning and say "I can't wait for my first failure of the day." If you do, well, let's just say you are different.

I think the key is to learn to separate ourselves from failure. If I do not get my dream job, it does not translate into me being a failure. If I do not lose the 15 pounds I wanted by the end of my diet, it does not translate into me being a failure. If I aim for a 4.0 GPA but achieve only a 3.5, I am definitely not a failure. Obviously, this is not easy to do.

I firmly believe that there is no single event in life that determines if someone is a success or failure. Unfortunately, however, our minds quickly jump to the conclusion of being a failure when we fall short of any goal we set. And far too often, this false extrapolation causes us to avoid taking the risk the next time we face an opportunity to take action. Many of us carry around permanent battle scars.

To truly accept accountability (as a verb), you have to take action. By taking action, you are taking a risk. In order to truly take the risk, you must be courageous and show vulnerability. You have to be willing to jump in the game with the attitude of "win, lose, or draw, I am giving it my best shot. And I will be better for it as a result, regardless of the outcome. I am going to aim for fulfillment instead of contentment!"

This point is so often demonstrated in sports. How many teams out there have no business being on the same field or court with the given opponent before the game ever begins? No one gives the team any chance at all of winning. The team is clearly just playing to fail - why play at all? (Images of David and Goliath come to mind and, of course, we all know what happened there.)

The most memorable example of this took place in the 1980 Winter Olympics in Lake Placid, New York. During the height of the Cold War with mounting tension between the United States (U.S.) and the former Soviet Union, the US hockey team had no chance at all of beating the mighty Russian team. Why even show up to play?

The U.S. team was filled with young college kids with very little playing time with each other, much less international experience. The Soviet team was filled with seasoned veterans who had played together for years, many of whom had already won gold medals in previous Olympics. On top of that, during the exhibition rounds before the Games, the Soviets defeated the Americans 10-3! Now, I do not know much about hockey, but when the score starts resembling a football score, I do know that the game can be classified as a blow out.

So here they were, David and Goliath, playing for the right for a place in the gold medal match. No one gave the Americans a chance; many feared embarrassment on the home soil in Lake Placid after such a humiliating loss in the exhibition match. The weight and pride of the entire country pressed down on the young Americans' shoulders. Obviously, fear of losing was not going to keep them from playing; however, fear of losing could keep them from giving their best and winning.

The American team, however, had no fear of losing. They were willing to take the supreme risk of standing up to the mighty Russians. They were willing to face defeat (and potentially humiliation) for the opportunity of victory. The result: probably the greatest moment in the history of American sport, probably one of the greatest upsets in sports history, probably one of best examples of the willingness to be courageous and take a risk for the better that we all aim to be. I remember the incredible feeling I had watching that moment although just 9 years old. I can only imagine the feeling of pride and exhilaration that team felt at that moment.

There are numerous other sports examples, such as N.C. State's improbably win over the Houston Cougars in the 1983 NCAA basketball championship or the 1988 World Series win by the L.A. Dodgers over the Oakland A's on the miraculous homerun in the bottom of the ninth by an almost cripple Kirk Gibson. In all of these examples, society basically told the underdog that they were the loser before the game ever began. In all of these examples, the underdog was given no chance for victory. Ironically, none of these underdogs believed anything other than that they could and would come out victorious. People will always remember Broadway Joe's infamous prediction that the underdog Jets would defeat the mighty Colts in Super Bowl III. And, of course, they did. Regardless of the great risk of failure, all of the so-called underdogs took the risk, stood up to the ugliness of potential defeat, and came out victorious. Why is this so hard for us to do sometimes in real life?

All of these examples share one thing beyond being sports examples. They all involve teams of people. It will always be much easier to take a risk with the support and synergy of a team than going at it all by your lonesome. Unfortunately, most of what we are discussing here involves you going at it all by your lonesome. Although this is true, I will challenge you later that none of us really have to face these risks alone.

Accepting accountability requires action...taking action for the better we want in life. Aiming for better requires all of us to leave our comfort zone of "steady as she goes" and take a risk. The risk comes from potentially losing the steady in favor of a worse place. However, we play this risk game for the potential of a much better place. This better place can be improved relationships, better health, more homeruns, a higher GPA, a more fulfilling career, or even a gold medal in the Olympics.

There is no magic bullet for taking the required risk. It is a matter of making up your mind and aligning all that you do (your behaviors) with the desires of your heart. And you have to do this with no fear of repercussions. No training course can teach you skills for doing this. It is a matter of convincing yourself that it is okay to fail and that the potential gain is well worth the risk of failing. You have to sincerely believe that failure in one of life's many events does not define you as a failure. No single event has the right to do this. We have all heard the story of the series of failures Abraham Lincoln faced before becoming President of the United States. Although he failed many times, he never defined himself as a failure. He kept pressing onward toward his ultimate goal. Later in the book, we will talk about another key to accepting accountability, but also key to taking risk, which is a belief in self.

I encourage you to aim for fulfillment versus contentment in all that you do. And, in doing so, you will truly be taking accountability for the better that you desire in life! I truly believe if you dig deep down into your inner self to explore the part that no one ever sees (and even you can barely see), there is a little voice that wants you to aim for fulfillment in life and not contentment. The question is will you listen and respond? Are you willing to be like Abraham Lincoln, the U.S. hockey team, Kirk Gibson, David, or any of the other multitudes of heroes in this world who refused to listen to society, took the risk, and came out victorious?

"Failure"

It's only a word. But it carries with it so much pain and so little concern, so much frustration and so little respect, so much stress and so little

understanding that people spend their lives running through their days in the hope of avoiding the long arm of this little word.

To test your vision, you must risk failure. To temper your ego, you must attempt the impossible. To tell your story, you must take a chance. To see beyond the horizon, you must spread your wings.

To be all you can be, you must stretch, flex, try, and go beyond your proven limits. To bridge the silence, you must risk rejection.

To advance into the unknown, you must risk the peril of all your previous beliefs and emotions that feel so secure.

Failure is not negative. It is a teacher. It molds, refines, and polishes you so that one day your light will shine for all to see.

It isn't the failure you experience that will determine your destiny, but your next step and then the next that will tell the story of your life.

-Tim Connor

CHAPTER FIVE

Accountability Anonymous Prayer

Needless to say, there are many things in life we cannot control. We cannot control the weather, death, or the passing of time. These things happen all around us every day with no consultation from any of us. We cannot control the behaviors of others, although there are plenty of circumstances in which we wish and even think we could. As the father of a four year old, I believe that the louder the tone of my voice, the greater control I have over Rick's behavior. Funny thing though, the louder I get, the more "opposite" his behavior seems to be from what I am aiming to achieve! No matter how hard you try, control of behaviors will always reside within the individual.

The Alcoholics Anonymous prayer is based on one by Reinhold Niebuhr. It is:

"God, grant me the serenity to accept the things I cannot change, courage to change the things I can, and the wisdom to know the difference."

This is one of the most powerful sayings I have ever read. It is asking for you to be at peace with the things you cannot control and to be courageous in attacking the things you can control. In reality though, how many of us behave this way? How many of us actually behave like this:

"God, help me to be content with myself, give me the ability to change the things I don't like about others, and the influence to help others know that I know what is best for them."

Sound familiar? We are all well equipped to cast the judging eye toward others and quick to shut our eyes when we look in the mirror. But this is just one part of completely understanding the Alcoholics Anonymous prayer.

There is but one thing we can control in life and that is our own behaviors. The only thing we control is that tiny space between stimulus and response that we discussed earlier. Unfortunately, the things we all want in life are outcomes...desired outcomes and that "better."

Outcomes in life are the result of the interaction of many factors. Our behaviors are just one of these factors. Timing, Mother Nature, the behaviors of others, and environmental factors are just some of the other inputs that ultimately determine our outcomes. As mentioned, we can only control our behaviors, which is but one of these influencing factors. Thus, in the prayer above, when you ask for serenity for those things you cannot change, you are asking for calmness in response to the outcomes you receive in life.

This is by far one of the toughest things to deal with in life. Having no control over the outcomes we experience is not something we want to accept. Now, don't get the wrong idea. I firmly believe that through the right behaviors, you can influence outcomes greatly, even to an extent where you can usually get what you are aiming for. But this will not always happen as you can only control your behaviors (an input) and not the outcomes (an output).

This is one of the greatest challenges I face every day in my own life. I am a control-freak. That is just how I am (and I am trying hard not to feel ashamed about it, but it felt good to show some vulnerability toward you). Fortunately, I learned early in my career through chance that I could wield great control over people by being an effective facilitator. Thus, for the last 10 years, about 90% of my career has been in facilitating teams of people to achieve a desired outcome. Now, assuming I am a pretty good facilitator, the teams of people never feel the control I have over them, but it is there. The key has always been control through influence and not power.

I have always believed that I could will things to happen. I remember as a kid watching one of those NFL Films shows. This particular one was highlighting the career of L.T. (Lawrence Taylor). In it, they showed clips from games and interviews with various teammates, opponents, and coaches. One of the comments focused on L.T.'s will. He had a relentless belief that he could will things to happen on the field. And it showed in that fact that in his prime, he could literally take over a football game and dictate many of its outcomes. In reality, it was L.T.'s behaviors on the field that caused the domination and the resulting outcome. The only thing L.T. really controlled was the behaviors he demonstrated in order to become one of the greatest linebackers in the history of the NFL. These behaviors led to greater preparation, greater intensity, and greater team leadership. All L.T. really controlled was his behaviors.

We each have many desired outcomes in life. For me, I want to live to be 100 years old. I want to think that I can control my son's behavior. I want to think that I can keep my wife's passion for shopping under control. I want to think that I can change the world. I want to think that for any desired outcome in my life, I can somehow will it to happen.

Unfortunately, that's not how it works. My challenge each day is to control the things that I can control (my behaviors) and align them with the things that I want to influence to change (my outcomes). This requires a paradigm shift since we are all taught at a very young age by society to focus on outcomes. Part of this is reflective of our materialistic culture. Outcomes are materialistic in nature. I am asking you to change your paradigm and focus on behaviors.

So I want to live to be 100 years old. I cannot control death and I have to accept this. If I truly accept this with serenity, I will live with no fear of dying. This outcome for which I have no control will just be treated as one of those inevitable things out there that will occur one day. What I can do, however, is a series of little things that will be part of the total equation that will determine when I will die. And if I align these little things with the desired outcome (live to be 100 years old), I am far more likely to live to 100 or beyond than if I just focused exclusively on the desired outcome.

These little things focus on my diet, daily exercise of the body/mind/heart, and other life-style choices that I make every day. My behaviors can be things such as never smoking, eliminating fried foods from my diet, and exercising for at least 30 minutes every day. These little things focus on all of those factors that I control that will influence how long I live.

What these little things will not include (but things that can/will play into determining when I die) are things such as worrying about what the other driver on the highway will do or whether or not the plane I am on will land safely. These little things will not include anything that I cannot control. Why should I waste time and energy (and sleepless nights) worrying about those things over which I have no control?

Although I want to control my son's behavior, I can only control my own. Although I need to accept this with serenity, by no means should I not aim to influence his behavior in order to help shape him into a person who believes in himself and is prepared to have a positive impact on society. In this case, my control should be on my effectiveness in loving and nurturing him. I should view my role as "coach" and ensure that I am coaching him through positive example. My focus should be on my influencing skills to ensure I help him see the differences between right and wrong. Once again, this is all that I can control. In the end, he must make decisions on his own and be held accountable. It is through my positive nurturing as a parent that I will hopefully influence him to make effective decisions and build strong character.

(On a side note, I have completely given up on ever influencing my wife's shopping habits. I am sure all you husbands out there know what I mean! When your wife starts telling you how much she saved versus how much she spent, you know that it is a lost cause.)

So what is the point of all of this and how does it relate to all this stuff about accountability?

We can only be accountable for our own behaviors and not the outcomes that result. This is very tough to accept, but I believe this is another key to truly accepting accountability for our personal success and achievement of our desired better. As mentioned in the last chapter, taking risk is key to getting better. The risk is that we may not get our desired outcomes. However, if we have the serenity to accept the things we cannot control (the outcomes), then we should also have serenity about risk. This is not easy by any means. This is saying we should be serene about "losing." Society has not conditioned us this way. We naturally try to avoid failures and the resulting wounds that come from them.

When things go wrong in your life, do you sulk about your behaviors or your outcomes? That is probably because most of our focus is on the outcomes, and it should not be. There is a ton of literature out there about performance metrics for organizations. Throughout my career, I have done quite a bit of research about how best to assess and report metrics in order to improve performance. One of the more insightful pieces of research I ever read described how to improve profit performance. Obviously, for all for-profit companies, earnings are a key measure of success and the ultimate desired outcome. However, this particular piece of research stated that companies should never focus on measuring profits because being the ultimate outcome, there was no way of directly controlling them. Thus, if you are a CEO or company owner, the focus should be on figuring out all of the things that exert key influence on profits within your company's environment and then focusing all of your energies on these. In the context of this book, these would be behaviors. What an interesting lesson! If you want the best profits (your outcomes), do not focus on them at all; focus all of your energies on the things that most influence profits (your behaviors).

This same lesson applies in our everyday lives. If you want the desired outcome (profits), focus all of your energies on figuring out the key behaviors that will have the greatest influence on obtaining the outcome. Once you know what these behaviors are, shift all of your energies toward living these behaviors every day. This can include behaviors that drive better relationships, better health, better grades, or better job performance.

The challenge comes when outcome day arrives. What if I fail? What if I made less "profit" than desired? Worse yet, what if I lose money? These undesired results can obviously occur, sometimes causing us not to play in this risky game the next time around. We receive what should be viewed as a minor wound and turn it into a permanent handicap.

The Alcoholic's Anonymous prayer tells us to say "so what?" You did not get the desired outcome and who cares! You did all you could. You figured out the behaviors needed and you fully demonstrated them every day. However, in the end, someone else's behaviors or Mother Nature or some other environmental factors kept you from winning. Should you feel ashamed? Should you quit? Are you now a failure? The answer to all of these questions is "Hell No!" (My choice of words is for emphasis only. My fear is having my mother read those words and be embarrassed as I do not think that she has ever even *thought* a "four letter word," much less said one out loud. Sorry Mom!!!)

The real risk we face in life is having things we cannot control (outcomes) keeping us from treating accountability as a verb. We cannot let potentially undesirable results keep us from taking action in life. It is kind of like this book. There is nothing in my experience or skill set that says I have any business writing a book. And as I struggle to put words together that seem logical, I laugh periodically about whether or not this book will ever make it to print, much less sell a copy. Does this mean I should not do this? Should I fear never being asked to be on the Today Show to talk about this book? And should this fear keep me from doing this? Absolutely not!

Failure does not come from outcomes. There are way too many factors that play into outcomes. Many of these we have zero control over. Somehow, we have to accept that fact with no regrets and with serenity. This is incredibly difficult to do since society teaches us to focus on outcomes. Unfortunately, outcomes are the things that get praised and rewarded.

When I think of the word serenity, I see myself lying on a beach with my eyes closed. My heart rate is about 40 beats per minute and I am at total peace with the world. Now, imagine the same feeling of serenity after you have laid it on the line to get a new promotion, but someone else got it. You did every possible thing you could to get this promotion. Every absolute thing you could control, you did right. Bottom line, though, the other candidate was a better choice. Do you feel ashamed, upset, disappointed, or serene? Feeling serene in this situation is incredibly difficult! To feel calm about any undesirable outcome when you have "laid it on the line" is asking a lot and in most cases impossible. It is, however, a critical element on your path toward truly accepting accountability.

I was once part of a very good football team that had a particular game circled on the schedule for months before the game ever arrived. We put every ounce of energy and preparation into this game. Unfortunately, we lost to a better team. There is no shame in this as we played a great game, the type of game you can use to build a great season. Unfortunately, our sole focus was on the outcome, and this game occurred very early in the year. The result was a losing record and no bowl game during a season in which we should have easily won 8-9 games out of the 11 we played.

An ole cliché in sports is to never let a loss beat you twice. In other words, you do not avoid the next game because you lost the previous. You do not avoid action because you are now afraid of the risk of losing. My hope would be that the defeat gives you greater resolve to increase your accountability and to take an even harder look in the mirror at yourself to see what you could have done differently in order to get your desired outcome the next time. It is asking a lot to be "serene" when you do not get the desired outcome you want. A more realistic aim is to never let a defeat in life beat you twice.

So, let's see if we can write a new prayer and call it the Accountability Anonymous Prayer:

"God, grant me the serenity to accept the outcomes I experience in life and help me to use them to learn and grow wiser; give me the courage to use that space between stimulus and response to create the better that I desire in my life and the vulnerability to treat accountability as a verb!"

None of this is easy. We all want to win and when we do not, we feel awful. We all hate losing, and society reinforces these feelings all the time. We do not take the time to celebrate the performance, instead focusing on rewarding the outcomes. When we do not get the outcomes desired, we lose sight of all that we gained from the experience that can be applied to even better performance in the future.

By no means should desired outcomes not play into our thinking and motivation; on the contrary, they should be the guiding light (later in the book, we will discuss "vision" and the critical role it plays in accountability). The desired outcomes should steer the behaviors of your daily journey. If not, you end up behaving a certain way for no reason at all. You end up "drifting" along in life. This form of stagnation will ultimately lead to regression. Without a sense of purpose and hope for better, it will become difficult to find the motivation to improve. Thus, outcomes do play a key role, but they just should not be the focus of our energies as you aim for better.

At the end of the day, who you are and what you are, your character, your personality, your "reflection", is completely defined by your behaviors. Your challenge is to not be fooled by society into thinking that you are defined by outcomes. If you do, then you will become a victim. You will always be in search of where to place blame for all of those outcomes that slip you by or fail to live up to expectations. As defined in our next chapter, you can absolutely never be a victim and accountable at the same time.

You Are Worthy
You are worthy of reaching for the greatest accomplishments.

And you are worthy of achieving them, no matter what other people think of you, no

matter what you have done up to this point in life.

You are worthy of the best.

You are unique, you are special.

You are creative and effective.

You have much value to offer, regardless of what anyone has told you.

And no one can express that value but you.

You are the person who deserves to live your dream.

You are the only one who has what it takes to reach that dream.

If you can see it, if you can imagine it, if you can dream it, you are worthy of reaching it.

And it is possible.

No one will hand it to you.

In fact, you'll strive day and night to reach it.

When you give the best you have, when you refuse to be stopped by the obstacles in your way, when you do what must be done, you'll get what you deserve—a full, rich life that is like no other.

Each day, with your thoughts and actions, live up to the fact that you are the best.

-Author Unknown

CHAPTER SIX

Can't Be A Victim

Today, upon a bus, I saw a very beautiful woman
and wished I were as beautiful.
When suddenly she rose to leave, I saw her hobble
down the aisle.
She had one leg and wore a crutch,
but as she passed, she passed a smile.
Oh God, forgive me when I whine. I have two legs; the
world is mine.

I stopped to buy some candy, the lad who sold it had
such charm.
I talked with him, he seemed so glad; if I were late, it'd
do no harm.
And as I left, he said to me, "I thank you, you have
been so kind. It's nice to talk to folks like you. You
see," he said, "I'm blind." Oh God, forgive me when I
whine. I have two eyes; the world is mine.

Later while walking down the street, I saw a child I
knew. He stood and watched the others play, but he
did not know what to do. I stopped a moment and
then I said, "Why don't you join them, dear?" He
looked ahead without a word. I forgot...he could not
hear. Oh God, forgive me when I whine. I have two
ears; the world is mine.

With feet to take me where I'd go. With eyes to see the sunset's glow. With ears to hear what I'd know. Oh God, forgive me when I whine. I've been blessed indeed, the world is mine.

-Anonymous

This is one of my all-time favorite poems and it speaks volumes about what it takes to truly be accountable. It clearly illustrates the fact that you cannot be a victim of life and accountable for your own life at the same time. You cannot go through life whining every time you do not get the outcomes you desire. Unfortunately, a terrible thing happens when you truly take accountability for self. There is no one left to blame but self when things go awry!

Far too often, we become victims and regress away from the better we are aiming for in life. As victims, we are basically blaming others or circumstances as the causes of our outcomes instead of taking personal accountability for them. By not taking this accountability, we typically use our space between stimulus and response to blame or say "Woe is me" instead of learning, adjusting, and taking action to achieve the better that we desire. If you use this space to "whine" as referenced in the poem above, you are not likely taking accountability and not likely to achieve true fulfillment. You have actually turned accountability for self over to others, resulting in zero control of your life and the better you desire. And none of us truly want this to happen.

More than anything else I can think of, having a victim mentality will keep you from succeeding. It will suck the life right out of your will to improve. It will create this false belief that you have no say in the outcomes in your life. It will become a self-fulfilling prophecy that says "hey, I am not accountable because there are just things out there against me. I am not in control; there is something out there that is in control and determining my destiny." This causes many to say, "hey, don't blame me." "They" did it to me. Who is this infamous "they" that gets blamed for so much in our lives? Even worse is when this mentality makes us say "why bother," causing us to not even try the next time.

There will always be a "they" out there and many times it will seem as though "they" are against you. But at the end of the day, "they" can absolutely never take away that space that exists between your stimulus and response. "They" can never control your behaviors. And regardless of how much it may seem "they" control things, "they" do not determine your true success in life. Remember, success should not be tied directly to outcomes but to how you respond to the circumstances you face in life. Your behaviors and your responses are all that you control and, thus, the true measure of your character and success in life. Let's take a look at some real life examples and see this come to life.

Ironically enough, one simple yet vivid example occurred today (literally the day I am typing these words on my laptop) in my own company. I had a co-worker who made a mistake. The manager of this person was involved in the situation, observed the mistake, and gave the person some feedback. Now, the manager did this in a public setting, which is not necessarily appropriate, but happens to be his style. This is how he always is and we all know it. Unfortunately, this led to embarrassment for my co-worker. I knew she was upset so I tried to comfort her. We discussed the situation and how this manager had handled it.

Now, the feedback shared was spot on; it was clear and valid. It hit home on some real improvement opportunities for my co-worker. However, my co-worker was a victim of the manager's style. Unfortunately, our entire post mortem focused on how the manager needed to change when it should have focused on accepting the manager as he is (give him credit for being consistent) and focus on what she could do differently going forward. But, in our discussion, there was no escaping her victim mentality and the desire to change everyone else, but not to look in the mirror at her flaws. Does this ever happen to you? You get some feedback, act defensively (a victim), and "rationally" figure out all the reasons why the feedback was not valid? This is the reaction of a victim, not someone who is accountable for self.

Throughout my career, I have worked directly for several executive-level leadership teams, teams that inevitably included people with heavy pedigrees, lots of degrees, and VP-type titles. It always amazed me how these highly paid and incredibly intelligent people would quickly become victims of the organization around them. All of these people had lots of power and authority, yet somehow felt powerless. The leadership within each of them had literally been sucked out of them by the "they" out there. I always wondered who the "they" really was. Ironically, in reality, "we" were actually "they!"

I remember vividly one particular circumstance where we were struggling with the current organizational design. We had just gone through the merger of two very large companies with strong cultures, and the current structure was quite cumbersome and duplicative. Decision making and information flow was quite confusing. It was a frustrating environment. There was no questioning this and even the most accountable person following all the principles outlined in this book would likely agree with this assessment. Fortunately, the organization did recognize this and the need for change. Unfortunately, the change process was quite political and slow to get moving toward something meaningful.

Time and time again, this particular leadership team spent countless hours literally whining about how "they" ("they" does not refer to the members of this team; this was this team referencing some infamous leadership group "out there" in the organization) did not communicate well or how "they" did not care what this team's members thought or how "they" were not listening to the organization or how "they" needed to help our people understand what was going on with this organizational change or simply how "they" needed to be more visible within the organization.

We literally spent a couple of hours at every one of our team meetings for well over six months wasting this time. It did not matter what I tried as a facilitator. The victim mentality always crept into the discussion and sucked the life out of our meetings. I recall numerous times trying to instill the mentality that "we are they," but there was no buying it. Too many of the team members were victims and they allowed this mentality to steal away their right to control that space between stimulus and response. Why couldn't "we" communicate better? Why couldn't "we" be more visible? Why couldn't "we" create small pockets of incremental change within our own organizations to bridge the gap from today's frustrations to tomorrow's better structure? Regardless of how much baiting I tried, there was no biting. These leaders were not willing to accept accountability, much less to treat it like a verb. They were victims and, as such, were not going to take action to make things better (treating accountability as a verb). There was plenty these folks still controlled (i.e. that space between stimulus and response), but the attitude remained "Woe is me" and "Why bother?"

For fun, I once did an analysis based on the number of hours we wasted, the likely hourly pay of these folks, and the number of people on our team to figure out how much money we literally threw away by virtue of this victim mentality. It was well over $100,000. Now, this may not seem like a lot of money, but what if all leadership teams across a large organization acted like this all of the time? It would add up to quite a large amount of lost productivity and profits all because people chose to be victims instead of accountable.

Their behavior represents such a scapegoat, such an easy way out. Things go bad and just forget about that mirror in your back pocket. It is "their" fault. "They" did it to me and "they" should be doing something different. "They" need to change. "They" are out to get me. Life just is not fair. Does any of this sound familiar?

Now, I know that I am just one person, but I think about how often I see this behavior all of the time in my own little world. Surely my world is not just a farfetched outlier on the radar screen? Think about how often you see these behaviors. What would a 50% reduction in them mean to our society?

How often does this victim mentality happen within your own life? I would challenge you to spend a day or week tracking how often you say (or even just think about) something or someone is "just not fair" or you place blame on something or someone for a negative outcome in your life. After tracking this, ask yourself what your responses would be if you acted accountably. What if you took your list and, for 50% of the items, you changed your response to "I am accountable" instead of "just not fair." Would you be happier, more successful, and more fulfilled?

Now, let's look at the polar opposite.

Have you ever known anyone who is blind person? If so, have you ever noticed that they always seem happy and fulfilled? This has always amazed me.

One blind person of my acquaintance is a man named "Jason." I have known him since he was a relatively young boy. He is truly an amazing person. From driving his granddaddy's truck to going coon hunting (and, of course, he handles taking care of his numerous coon dogs), he leads a fairly normal life. There are a lot of amazing things to say about "Jason", but the thing I will always remember is how he knew people who came to his house before they entered as he learned to recognize car sounds. He could always recognize my father's truck. He could also recognize keys to different types of cars. For example, he could distinguish between a Ford and Chevy.

"Jason", like many blind people or those with other types of handicaps, had a very special gift that we could all do well to learn. Instead of measuring happiness and fulfillment by "immaterial" things such as money, looks, or power, he measured happiness and fulfillment by character, with character meaning to live life to the fullest with the gifts and talents you have. It does not matter what these gifts and talents are as most of us have absolutely no say in the gifts and talents we "inherit" when we are born. What matters is that we use them, nurture them, and maximize their potential regardless of what they are.

If there was one thing about "Jason" that stands out, he was always happy...smiling, telling jokes, "picking" on himself and others. He was an inspiration to everyone around him. He could have easily and understandably been a victim. He was dealt a bad hand and no one would blame him if he whined. But, heroes do not respond this way. You see, "Jason" has the same right we do to that space between stimulus and response. He has decided to use this space to say "hey, I might be blind, but there is absolutely nothing I can do about this. I can still choose how I respond to this and I choose to live my life to the fullest and do the things I want to do, including going coon hunting, regardless of my circumstances!"

God did not bless "Jason" with eye sight, and "Jason" easily blamed God, whined, and said "oh, woe is me!" Instead, "Jason" said "so what?" God blessed "Jason" with a beautiful heart, a love for the outdoors, and a relentless attitude to never behave as though he were handicapped. It is kind of ironic how quickly we "non-handicapped" folks try to label handicapped people and make special concessions for them. Ironically, people who are handicapped never want to be treated differently. When you think about people like "Jason," it makes you wonder who the actual handicapped people are: those like Jason or those who "whine" and are victims of the "they" out there. When it comes to living life to the fullest and taking accountability for self, are the "Jasons" of this world the real handicapped or the team of VPs I referenced earlier?

Now, I am sure the "Jasons" of our world do have fears. It is completely normal for all of us to have fears. But I am reminded of a quote that I heard on one of those old NFL Films movies ("Crunch Course") during a scene where they were talking about players who cover kick-offs. Now, if you know anything about football, you know that the people who cover kick-offs are from a different planet. They are today's version of Kamikaze pilots. Their jobs are pretty simple: run 50-60 yards as fast as you possibly can and ram your body with all your might into anything between you and the person with the ball. They were interviewing a military officer in comparing frontline soldiers with football players who cover kick-offs for a living. He called them all the "real heroes," meaning that the real heroes are those who are truly afraid, but they do it anyway. "Jason" may have been afraid every day he awakened in darkness (I know I would be). But he lives life to the fullest anyway. He is a real hero.

There are countless heroes like "Jason" in this world. Ironically, while writing this chapter, I came upon the name "Lacey Heward." I had no idea who she was, but she was staring me in the face while I drank a soda from McDonalds. Her face and bio were on the cup. This struck my interest so I decided to do some research.

I "googled" her and got over 1,000 hits. What I found was someone who was the victim of a childhood accident that left her paralyzed. When she was just 16 months old, a 100-lb. dumbbell fell off a weight bench and crushed her back, leaving her disabled. So, how did she go from this tragic circumstance to being on the cup of soda I was drinking?

The answer is pretty simple. She was accountable and not a victim. Today, she is a *world champion* skier. Her next goal in life is pretty simple as she aims to win a gold medal at the 2006 Paralympics. Here is yet another example of someone who is a hero and not a victim.

How easy would it have been for Lacey to lead a very sheltered life? She could have easily felt sorry for herself and no one would have blamed her. How many of us would have responded the way she did to the type of circumstances she faced? Her family and society would have pampered her every need, leaving her completely dependent. Instead, look at her know on a cup of soda at McDonalds. This is pretty amazing stuff, but it is also as simple as her simply using that space between stimulus and response to say "I am accountable and I choose differently. I am not a victim. I may not have the best of circumstances, but I will live my life to the fullest and I will be successful."

How many of us with no real handicaps actually "handicap" ourselves from reaching our fullest potential? Lacey is going for a gold medal while we "handicapped" people whine about what "they" did to us. Lacey says to life "bring it on" and we stand still while blaming others for our circumstances.

It is really amazing to think about these types of stories. For these people, outcomes do not matter; it is just the fact that they chose to not be a victim to something they had absolutely ZERO control over. Their behaviors made all the difference.

Have you ever volunteered for the Special Olympics and seen how happy those folks are just to compete?

And, yet how often do we not respond this way to circumstances much easier than what the "Jasons" and Laceys of this world face? Once again, we need to ask God to forgive us when we whine. I know we sometimes do not realize it and many times we do not want to hear it, but we are all richly blessed in someway. If in no other way, we each have life and, by virtue of that space between stimulus and response (another blessing), we can shape what life brings us. We may have limitations that we cannot control, but so what? We still completely control how we respond to these limitations. It is our own choice to be a victim or a hero.

Regardless of circumstances, we all have the right to that space between stimulus and response. "Jason" owns that space, Lacey owns that space, and Victor Frankl owned that space. Remember his story from earlier? Another real hero, he used this space to overcome the trials and tribulations of a Nazi concentration camp. Ironically, although society may try to make us think differently, none of these real heroes had special degrees, pedigrees, or other physical/material attributes that made them special. They each had the same basic blessings that we each have (the space granted between every stimulus and our responses), but they chose to use these blessings in a very special way. Their behaviors made them special and the last time I checked, all behaviors are the truest of commodities. As commodities, this means that having them and using them requires no special degrees, pedigrees, or skills. They are ours for the taking.

While in that space between stimulus and response, we each face that moment of truth where we choose to either be a victim or a hero. If we are truly accountable, we view this space as our opportunity to make a difference within our own lives and those of the people around us. Regardless of the circumstances, regardless of the environment, regardless of what the other person does, this is our space to define who we are, where we have been, and where we are headed. "Jason" uses this space to go coon hunting with his friends who each have two perfectly functioning eyes that can actually see the targets. Lacey Heward uses this space to prepare to win a gold medal. Victor Frankl used this space to not only survive, but thrive under the worst imaginable physical and emotional circumstances.

How do you use this space? Do you use this space to say "Woe is me?" Do you use it to place blame? Do you use it to whine? Do you use it to make excuses? Or do you use it to learn and grow, to map your better tomorrow, and to truly be accountable by treating it like a verb?

I do not want to make things seem easier than they really are in real life. Life is tough, filled with challenging and complex decisions, pressures from all directions, and countless forces that may seem to be out to get you. However, at the end of the day, you still own that space between stimulus and response. It is still and always will be this space which determines your success in life. It is up to you if you choose to be a victim or choose to be a hero. Both choices are completely within your control. Every day, you decide how often you will whine.

So, you have a simple self-assessment to complete. We all say "why" many times throughout every day of our lives. This is completely normal and neither good nor bad. It just is. The assessment is to figure out the type of punctuation you typically put after the word "why." If you end it with a "?" then you are doing exactly what you should be doing to ensure constant growth in your life. If you accept undesired outcomes as they are and never question why, then you will never grow. Asking the question enables you to explore how to do things differently in the future to drive better outcomes. However, far too often, we do not end "why" with a "?" Instead, we emphatically end the word "why" with a resounding "!" Get the difference? I would challenge that those who constantly learn and grow and ultimately succeed in life almost always ask the question "why?" Those of us who are stuck in a rut or who struggle with the things we cannot control make the statement "why!" Those of us who are making the statement "why!" are whining as a victim would. So, for the next few days or weeks, keep track of how many "!" versus "?" you use after the word "why." Then, set a goal to change the ratio to more "?" versus "!" and see if does not start to have a dramatic impact on your outcomes.

> Today, upon a bus, I saw a very beautiful woman
> and wished I were as beautiful.
> When suddenly she rose to leave, I saw her hobble
> down the aisle.
> She had one leg and wore a crutch,
> but as she passed, she passed a smile.
> Oh God, forgive me when I whine. I have two legs; the
> world is mine.
>
> I stopped to buy some candy, the lad who sold it had
> such charm.

I talked with him, he seemed so glad; if I were late, it'd do no harm.
And as I left, he said to me, "I thank you, you have been so kind. It's nice to talk to folks like you. You see," he said, "I'm blind." Oh God, forgive me when I whine. I have two eyes; the world is mine.

Later while walking down the street, I saw a child I knew. He stood and watched the others play, but he did not know what to do. I stopped a moment and then I said, "Why don't you join them, dear?" He looked ahead without a word. I forgot...he could not hear. Oh God, forgive me when I whine. I have two ears; the world is mine.

With feet to take me where I'd go. With eyes to see the sunset's glow. With ears to hear what I'd know. Oh God, forgive me when I whine. I've been blessed indeed, the world is mine.

-Anonymous

CHAPTER SEVEN

Need A Vision

SAIL, DON'T DRIFT

I find the greatest thing in this world not so much where we stand, as in what direction we are moving. To reach the port, we must sail sometimes with the wind, and sometimes against it, but we sail, and not drift, nor live at anchor.

--O. W. Holmes

Truly being accountable is all about treating the word as a verb. It is all about taking action for the things you want to change and to create better within your life. This is not easy as you must be willing to take risks in order to give up on your current state of contentment to obtain a better state of fulfillment. This takes great vulnerability on your part. You have to be willing to show your "stains" to the world without shame or regret. It also takes an ability to truly understand what you can control versus those things that you can't. This takes a shift in thinking to focus on behaviors and not outcomes, which run counter to what society has taught us to do. Throughout this process, you must avoid being a victim. You cannot let those forces "out there" that seem to be against you keep you from taking action. Whining is definitely not part of the accountability equation.

None of this is easy. I actually believe that it is almost impossible to be accountable for self without a vision for self. Now, when I say "vision," I am not necessarily talking about those fancy things that some Fortune 500 companies have plastered all over their facilities. What I am talking about is a deeply seeded purpose for your life that serves as the foundation for all that you do. It is the motivation that gives meaning to your actions and provides fuel for your accountability. It would be very difficult for me to be accountable for anything if what I was doing (my actions) was not driven by a greater cause...a purpose and vision. Vision simply answers the questions "What do you want to get out of life?", "How do you want to be remembered", and "What do you want your legacy to be?"

Visions are usually associated with organizations. And many have outstanding visions. The ones I like are those tied to purpose and values instead of outcomes. Outcomes to me represent an ending and I think vision should reflect a journey, not a destination. (I say this and yet my personal vision includes some specifics that reflect somewhat of a destination. Such a hypocrite am I!)

One of my favorite "visions" comes from Johnson & Johnson. Now, theirs is not the typical, generalized, and "not saying a whole lot" vision statement. It is called their "Credo." For over 60 years, this statement of purpose has existed and guided the company's every action. Obviously, the situation that most of us outside of the company know about is the Tylenol incident from over 20 years ago, when seven people in the Midwest died after taking Tylenol tablets from bottles that had been laced with cyanide.

As soon as investigators linked these mysterious deaths to

Extra-Strength Tylenol (the product of a Johnson & Johnson subsidiary), the company gave up profits in order to immediately do the right thing. In today's environment, you hear so much negative press of unethical behavior in the name of profits that it is nice to see examples of companies who have a greater purpose that drives their accountability. At Johnson & Johnson, the Credo demands accountability and creates a clear sense of purpose for all employees. Read the Credo below and see the clear purpose and core values of the organization throughout the words.

We believe our first responsibility is to the doctors, nurses and patients,
to mothers and fathers and all others who use our products and services.
In meeting their needs everything we do must be of high quality.
We must constantly strive to reduce our costs
in order to maintain reasonable prices.
Customers' orders must be serviced promptly and accurately.
Our suppliers and distributors must have an opportunity
to make a fair profit.
We are responsible to our employees,
the men and women who work with us throughout the world.
Everyone must be considered as an individual.
We must respect their dignity and recognize their merit.
They must have a sense of security in their jobs.
Compensation must be fair and adequate,
and working conditions clean, orderly and safe.
We must be mindful of ways to help our employees fulfill
their family responsibilities.
Employees must feel free to make suggestions and complaints.
There must be equal opportunity for employment, development
and advancement for those qualified.
We must provide competent management,
and their actions must be just and ethical.
We are responsible to the communities in which we live and work
and to the world community as well.

We must be good citizens – support good works and charities
and bear our fair share of taxes.
We must encourage civic improvements and better health and education.
We must maintain in good order
the property we are privileged to use,
protecting the environment and natural resources.
Our final responsibility is to our stockholders.
Business must make a sound profit.
We must experiment with new ideas.
Research must be carried on, innovative programs developed
and mistakes paid for.
New equipment must be purchased, new facilities provided
and new products launched.
Reserves must be created to provide for adverse times.
When we operate according to these principles,
the stockholders should realize a fair return.

Now, do I believe that in order for you to be effective in your battle to truly accept accountability that you need to go out and draft a multiple paragraph purpose for your life? Absolutely not! Do you need to put something on paper? Not necessarily. However, I firmly believe that in order to be effective in your accountability, you need to do some soul searching to know what is truly important to you and, in turn, be true to yourself by letting this drive your actions. Whether or not you put it on paper is up to you. For Johnson & Johnson, its Credo led to a specific behavior to pull Tylenol off every store shelf regardless of the financial impact until the company knew that it would no longer harm people. Actions were clear and swift. This is a great example of accountability as a verb.

Long paragraphs are not required to create a sense of purpose. Walt Disney created a simple yet compelling vision for his company that has withstood the test of time. He stated, "We are in the happiness business." At Disney, it is all about creating magic for people. Might sound odd, but every time I enter the gates at one of the Disney theme parks, I cannot help but be transformed into a kid again. It always feels like I have entered an entirely different world. The simple statement by Walt Disney still drives everything that takes place with the company and you can see, smell, hear, and touch it everywhere you look. And this also gives a clear sense of accountability to all who work at Disney.

My personal vision is pretty simple as I have stated previously. I want to live to be 100 years old. When I die, I want to go to Heaven. While alive, I want to be the absolute best husband and father that I can be. That's really it. This provides me with the clarity that I need to make decisions and take actions on a daily basis to act accountably for self. If truly accountable, all that I do will align with this vision. It will be my motivation to take action and serve as my guiding light when I am in that space between stimulus and response.

I fully realize that I said vision should be more of a journey than a destination. Clearly, 100 years old and Heaven are destinations so I fully accept any criticism you have for me. I cannot help it, though. This is my vision! You see, I love living my life with my wife and want as many years of this as I can have. Unfortunately for me, the women on my wife's side of the family live a long, long time. Her grandmother died right before turning 100 and her great-aunt is still kicking at 104 years old! If I thought Betsy would die before 80, maybe my vision would be different, but as it stands, if I live to 100, Betsy will be 103. So, I like the odds of my vision being pretty close to the right target. Heaven as part of my vision is simply a reflection of my Christian beliefs.

So, how is all of this tied to truly accepting accountability? I think the answer lies in motivation. Accepting accountability is not easy. As we have already discussed, the easy way out is to be a victim. It is much easier to go through life complaining and singing the blues of "Woe is me!" Further, it is lots more fun to be critical of others than to hold up the mirror and see the ugliness of self. Finally, contentment requires so much less effort than fulfillment. The bottom line of all of this is that not truly accepting accountability requires so much less effort on my part, is easier, and less risky. Why would I not want this? Why put so much pressure on myself just to be accountable?

Hopefully, the answer lies in my vision as it should aim for something better. My vision is something I can see out there in the future, a picture of myself in a new and better place. Obviously, the vision should be compelling (motivating) to fuel my actions. If truly motivating, my vision makes me want more and more out of my life. It makes me accountable for all of my actions and behaviors and, ultimately, where I am headed.

Let's take a look at my vision. I want to live to be 100 years old. Obviously, a key determining success factor of this is my health. So, if I look at my health, there are some things I cannot control. My grandfather and father both had/have type I diabetes. Now, diabetes is a highly inheritable genetic disease and there is a strong chance that I could have type I diabetes. (My father was 35 when he found out he had the disease. Ironically, as I write this, I am 34 years old.) There is absolutely nothing I can do about this. Reflecting on the Accountability Anonymous prayer, I need to accept this. There is no need to whine.

However, all of my behaviors related to my health I fully control. What I eat, how often I run, and the intensity of my anaerobic workouts are completely in my control. The right choices in these areas are not fun. It is much more fun eating a 50-wing platter from Hooters than avoiding fried foods. It is much more fun crashing on the couch when I get home from work than going for my evening run. Inevitably, the non-accountable route is easier and so much more fun. I would love to simply be a victim of all of the great desserts in the world and then just whine about my waistline!

So how do I overcome the fun and easy way out? The answer is my vision. Living to be 100 years old is compelling and motivates me to take full accountability for my physical health. It fuels actions that drive my better health. Every day, I have a series of spaces between each stimulus and response that relate to my health. Simple actions I take are things such as running six days a week, lifting weights seven days a week, and avoiding certain foods as much as possible (things like butter, mayonnaise, and fried foods...anything that has fat written all over it).

Just to be controversial, I am a firm believer that maximum physical health (the full picture, not just weight control) comes from a strong and balanced focus on aerobic exercise, weight lifting, balanced diet (with a strong focus on proteins and carbs), and proper sleep. These fad diets that talk about eating lots of fats while minimizing carbs are crazy for proper health. You have got to do the right amount of exercise, which needs to include intense aerobic work, to push the heart to its limits. If you are minimizing the fuel you need to exercise (carbs) and build your muscles (protein), you will fall short of your total health goals. Now, if your goal is simply to lose weight, more power to you. Go with the fad diet if that works for you. But I believe the real vision should be better health and not just to lose weight. Better health requires more than the fad diet. If you are truly accountable for your health, you go beyond just the right diet and focus on maximum physical health.

For my physical health, treating accountability as a verb requires daily actions, not just words that say I am accountable. It requires discipline and daily actions that reflect my vision to live to be 100 years old. If I want to live to be 100, I better be doing all that I can every day to keep a healthy heart, healthy muscles, and healthy bones. It goes beyond just maintaining a certain weight. Living to be 100 years old has to be a genuine and compelling purpose in my life to truly motivate me to make the tough over the easy/fun choices on a daily basis.

Another part of my vision is to be the absolute best husband I can be. Obviously, this is a journey. I will never achieve this desired state. (I imagine there are plenty of times my wife thinks I am not even in the right area code.) However, it does motivate me to be truly accountable for my effectiveness as a husband.

If I am truly accountable for my effectiveness as a husband, I treat this accountability as a verb. Thus, I treat my love for Betsy as a verb. I must take daily actions to truly love her. This is not easy either. Lots of times it is much easier just to treat this accountability as a noun. Can't I just do the simple things like tell her I love her and remember the "big" holidays with some flowers? Absolutely not! Every day presents opportunities between stimulus and response to renew my love for her at an entirely deeper level. How I use these spaces defines how much I truly love loving my wife.

Accountability as a verb in this situation can take many forms. And the key comes back squarely to my behaviors. It is never about what Betsy needs to do differently. It must always focus on what I need to do differently, the actions I need to take. (Obviously, the real key to a successful relationship that truly renews itself every day is one where both partners act this way.) What can I do this day, at this moment, to treat love as a verb in our relationship?

I firmly believe it is all about the little things. It is about taking the time to "read" her needs and when she just needs me to listen, I truly listen. It is about little surprises and knowing those things that make her feel special and acting on these. (For Betsy, this is easy. It is the 3 C's...anything related to clothes, coffee, or chocolate.) For example, if I need to run to the store to get gas, I simply run inside the convenience store and buy her a Starbuck's frappuccino (with some flavors of this drink, I hit 2 C's with just one purchase. With practice, you figure these things out). When I get home, she gets that little giddy smile that says she has felt my love for her. It is a little thing, but it is an action reflecting my accountability for aiming to be the absolute best husband I can be. Although a small thing, it says "I Love You" much louder than just the words by themselves. This little act tells her she is special to me.

Obviously, the key to any successful relationship is a win-win mentality. The challenge lies in knowing that the only thing

I can control in my part of the win-win is my own behaviors. I think too many relationships fail because of one of two scenarios. The first is when one of the partners spends all day being critical of the other partner and never holding up the mirror to self. There is no real accountability for the success of the partnership. It is all about what *you* need to do differently to please *me!* The other scenario is when one is the victim of the behaviors of the other. The other partner completely dominates the relationship and the first partner becomes a victim of this, tying all of his/her worth in the relationship to the happiness/worth of that other partner. Win-win will never be achieved if criticism and selflessness (victim) are key characteristics of the so-called partnership.

At the end of the day, I am not in my relationship with Betsy for some philanthropic reason to bring happiness to her life. I am in it because of the happiness and fulfillment it brings me in return. Of course, my happiness and the success of the relationship is anchored in her happiness and fulfillment. Remember, it is all about win-win. But do not fool yourself. There has to be some selfishness in order for win-win to truly occur. You have to win too!

I can go on and on about how my vision is the key motivator for my accountability. If I want to live to be 100 years old, I better have a plan for the financial security of my "golden years." This accountability does not begin when I start approaching retirement age. It begins today, even yesterday. I am very fortunate to be married to a CPA, someone who takes a very disciplined approach to financial planning. Thus, we are quite the obsessive couple when it comes to analyzing cash flows and making future financial projections. Regardless of how we could be viewed, there are some really simple actions we take that demonstrate our accountability and make a real difference. These include such things such as maximizing our company matching 401K benefits, having zero tolerance for credit card interest charges (if we cannot pay it off in the current month or directly with cash, we simply do without), and simply thinking about retirement projections (financial calculators are cheap and easy to use). Once again, the motivation for these actions comes back to the motivation of the vision to live to be 100. Having to deal with the stresses of financial burdens is not something that helps you live longer. Thus, I want to do all that I can today to avoid these types of stressors later in life.

Now, I know some people will say that they do not understand complex accounting lingo. That is completely fair. But remember accountability is not about knowledge, it is all about action. In this case, there are plenty of actions you can take. Explore the Internet, talk to friends/colleagues who understand finances, make an appointment with a financial advisor or planner, talk to your bank, take an introductory finance course, or buy that financial calculator. There are numerous actions you can take to demonstrate your accountability for your financial security. The bottom line is that if you are truly accountable, you will find an action to take. Unfortunately, doing nothing is also taking action, just not a wise choice!

So, let's go back to the beginning. Truly being accountable requires all of us to take the road that is not the fun and easy route. It requires action, it requires vulnerability, and it requires risk. I believe that in order to ever do anything that requires an action on my part that involves risk and vulnerability, there must be an underlying motivator that is more compelling than all of the voices asking me if I am crazy. I believe the strength of this motivation has to be rooted in a compelling vision for where I want to be headed in my life…the better that I am searching for.

If this vision is missing, it will be all too easy to not go running on that cold and rainy afternoon. It will be all too easy to make that second trip through the buffet line. It will be all too easy to go through the motions with your partner versus treating love as a verb in your relationship. And, as these easy way outs occur, they will become habits. Habits are so easy to form, yet so hard to break. Vision is vital to avoid the unwanted slippage into bad habits.

Your vision does not have to be good enough for a Harvard Case Study. It does not have to be written for that matter (although I think anytime you take something from your mind and put it on paper, you will discover it anew and it will become clearer to you). It just needs to be true to your innermost values, beliefs, and motives. It has to be true to you. This is not easy and it takes time to truly understand you. But no one has the chance to truly know you more than you!

How do you know when you get it "right?" In reality, I believe you will know it every day. If you feel fulfilled in life, you are likely aiming in the right direction on the journey toward the better that you desire. If truly fulfilled, you are likely holding yourself accountable (as a verb) for moving toward your vision every day. This may seem soft and fuzzy, but in reality, you are the only one who can judge your own personal happiness and fulfillment. As I have stated before, when it comes to accountability, the buck stops with you. You are in control of your accountability and your vision. What fulfillment looks like for you is unique to you. Now, do not sell yourself short, but, at the end of the day, you define what this looks like.

Deep Inside
Standing on the beach, sand between my toes
What lays in my future, who will come and go
The sun beams down upon me, as I raise my head and look
At the vast ocean before me, its size which I mistook
I feel so insignificant compared to this great expanse
What difference can I make, will I even be given a chance
I realize then while standing there, that all I have to do
Is listen to my heart and it will pull me through
For strength and inspiration are not material things
They come from deep inside of you they give your soul its wings
So whenever you're in doubt and you begin to stray
Take a look down deep inside and the answer will come your way
If you only believe in yourself you can make your dreams come true
For no one else can do it, the power must come from you
-Taylor Duncan

If there is any question in your mind and heart about being fulfilled, then I think you need to take a hard look at both your vision and whether or not you are treating accountability as a verb in life. Do you have a sense of purpose? Are you being true to your heart's desires? Do you catch yourself "whining" and saying "Woe is me?" Do you catch yourself being critical of others but never taking out that mirror to evaluate your own self? The answers to these questions are critical as you evaluate where you are, decide what changes you need to make, and, most importantly, the actions you take as a result of this reflection.

This is quite a weight to place on your shoulders. But you really have no choice if you want better in your life. Better requires accountability treated as a verb! In order to carry this burden successfully, you must have a strong belief in self. This is not at all about cockiness or arrogance. This is all about knowing that we are all special with unique tools/skills/personalities to make a difference in this world. We all have a legacy to leave, but it must be discovered (vision) and acted upon (accountability). No one can do this for you. It is completely up to you. As humans, we are uniquely endowed to freedom of choice. Remember Frankl? Most would think that he was not "free" by any stretch of the imagination, but he exercised freedom of choice every day in that horrific death camp. We are all in much better places than he was. But the question remains if you will choose not only to exercise, but maximize your freedom of choice.

The next chapter dives into this critical enabler of belief in self.

CHAPTER EIGHT

Belief In Self

As mentioned many times already, truly accepting accountability as a verb within your life is not easy. It is actually downright challenging, requiring a combination of risk taking, vulnerability, and humility. It takes constant effort and a great deal of confidence to pull this off. You really have to trust yourself to do this effectively. You have to have a strong sense of self-worth. Self-worth is something that ultimately has to come from you. Others can praise you and try to pump you up, but, at the end of the day, you have to decide that you are worthy.

You And Yourself
It is rewarding to find someone whom you like, but it is essential to like yourself. It is quickening to recognize someone as a good and decent human being, but it is indispensable to view yourself as acceptable.
It is a delight to discover people who are worthy of respect, admiration, and love, but it is vital to believe yourself deserving of these things.
For you cannot live in someone else. You cannot find yourself in someone else. You cannot be given a life by someone else. Of all the people you will know in a lifetime, you are the only one you will never leave nor lose.

To the question of your life, you are the only answer.
To the problems of your life, you are the only solu-
tion.
-Anonymous

At the end of the day, you are the only answer and the
only solution. As I have mentioned before, the accountability
buck stops with you. Self-worth is foundational to being able to
take the leap of faith into truly accepting accountability. This
self-worth leads to a strong belief in self and personal value.
With belief in self, I am not talking about confidence that leads
to swelling self-pride. Swelling self-pride can easily lead to bad
outcomes such as cockiness, which can run counter to your desire to enhance your effectiveness. Cocky people have an incredibly difficult time being effective in an interdependent world.
So, there has to be the proper balance of self-confidence with
humility.

Humility is all about having a strong confidence in self
without thinking you are any better than anyone else. Cockiness is when this confidence starts making you think you are
better than others and having to show it to others. Humility
is all about being grounded, having confidence in your abilities
yet a firm understanding of your limitations. Cockiness is when
you ignore your limitations and exaggerate your abilities. Cockiness also focuses heavily on talking the talk, whereas humility
focuses on walking the walk with no one needing to know that
you are walking. As long as humility is present, I do not think
cockiness will be an issue for you. Ironically, I strongly believe
that cockiness is a sign of weakness and that humility is a sign
of strength. Funny, though, how society does not teach us to
behave this way!

What I am talking about here is a solid belief in your self-worth. I am a firm believer that "God don't make any crap!" We all have value and unique abilities to make a difference in this world. We are all blessed with skills and opportunities to create better for both ourselves and the lives of the people we interact with every day.

Unfortunately, too many of us do not believe in our self-worth. We lack that confidence to believe that we can create better. We have either allowed society or ourselves individually to convince us that we do not have self-worth, or at least not enough to truly "go for it!" This false belief causes us to either turn down or ignore opportunities that are presented to us in that space between stimulus and response. Too often we listen to all of those victims out there and they convince us to be victims as well!

Do a quick exercise for me. Make a list of every reason you have for not believing in your self-worth. This can include anything you do not like about yourself or other limitations you believe you have that keep you from fulfilling your dreams.

How many of the items on the list are things you have absolutely zero control over (and should not waste another second worrying about)? How many are things that you created through your own behaviors (and, thus, through your own behaviors can change them to where you want them to be at any time of your choosing)? I would be willing to bet all of my own self-worth that every single thing on your list fell into one of these two categories. The items are either things we have zero control over or things we have complete control over. I have already talked about the need to let go of those things you cannot control.

Regarding the other part of the list, you have complete control to make a change today. And you have the self-worth to do so at this very moment if you are willing!

Your self-worth should never be tied to things you cannot control. In reality, self-worth is something you are born with; it is an entitlement by virtue of being human. In turn, this can never be taken away from you. Unfortunately, we all too often lose sight of it and think we have lost it. Luckily, our self-worth does not depreciate in value, but quite often goes under-realized and under-utilized.

Now, going back to your list, how many items did you classify as having no control over at all? Think deeply about your own behaviors. Is there absolutely nothing that you can do to control these things or at least influence them to some degree? How many of these items did you classify as "no control" when, in reality, if you had a stronger sense of self-worth, you could and would do something (your behaviors) to change them? How often do you sell yourself short? How often do you set artificial limitations because you simply believe you cannot change the outcome? Obviously, "victims" are more prone to having a larger percentage of their list as "zero control" and spend countless hours "whining" away precious moments that could be used to exert some influence to change these circumstances.

Now, let's look back on some of our examples from earlier (the Adam Morrisons, the Jasons, the Lacey Hewards, the Victor Frankls of this world). Do you think they had a self-worth problem? On their lists from above, do you think there were lots or few items that they said they had zero control over? I am willing to bet they had few if any. There is nothing special per se about this confidence, yet it is so rare.

I say that it is not special because we each can have it. A sense of self-worth does not require a graduate degree from Harvard or a certain look or a certain pedigree. It is something deep inside each of us that we individually have to let out of its cage.

So how do we let this sense of self-worth out of its cage? That is an incredibly difficult question to answer. If I knew the exact answer, I could make a large sum of money by bottling it up and selling it on the street corner. I do believe, however, that it all begins with loving yourself first and foremost. Learning to love yourself is the first step toward trusting yourself, which will lead to confidence.

We are all taught very early in life to not be selfish and to think about the needs of others before our own. Both of these points are important and necessary for success in operating in an interdependent society. But I do not believe you can truly love another or give to another until you learn to love yourself and take care of yourself by giving to yourself. And I do not believe that these points are in conflict with one another. They are actually complementary and interdependent. Loving self does not have to mean you are selfish. Taking care of yourself does not mean you are treating your needs as more important than the needs of others.

So, how does one go about loving oneself? Well, I think it starts with being true to yourself. Your values and beliefs should be reflected in all that you do every day. If you want to be an artist but allow family pressures to convince you to stay in the family business doing something totally different, your self-worth (and happiness) will likely suffer. You are not being true to yourself. If your values say one thing but your actions say another, there will be conflict inside. And this conflict will keep you from loving yourself. You will be filled with doubt, regret, and, in some cases, depression if you fail to be true to your values. I always find it interesting that whenever I do something I should not (that runs counter to my values), my conscience tells me. My conscience actually knows me better than I know me and lets me know whenever I am acting out of line with my values. I just need to learn to listen better to my conscience in order to find greater insights into my true values.

Earlier in my career, I was a career counselor for an outplacement firm. I was working with a client who was struggling with her career and wanted to make a change. We went through the standard procedures (various personality tests, skills inventories, etc.) to explore where she really wanted to go professionally. Everything kept pointing her in the current direction, which confused her more because she was not happy at all and thought dramatic change was needed. As we discussed her current situation on a deeper level, we finally found the answer. She was actually very happy with the type of work she was doing, but she was being asked to do something in particular by her boss that ran counter to her values and beliefs. This was the root of her unhappiness, but it was such an "ah-ha" experience for her. By giving in to her boss's request, she was not being true to herself and this was having a detrimental effect on her happiness and sense of self-worth. Needless to say, we worked hard at finding her a new boss in order to rekindle her self-worth.

Knowing self (your values, beliefs, etc.) takes time. If you were lucky, you kind of just knew what you wanted to be when you grew up from an early point in life. (I am not just talking about career here, but all elements of who and what you want to become.) But, for most of us, this is a long-term process of discovery. For others, it may be a never-ending journey. In reality, however, these values and beliefs are usually right in front of our faces for our own discovery. Unfortunately, we are either too blind, too busy, or in denial to truly discover them. Too often, we fail to listen to our conscience.

Think about those times in life when you really felt happy and fulfilled. What were you doing? What feelings did you have inside? Were you exhilarated? Did you have that permanent grin on both outside and, more importantly, inside? Most likely, these times reflected your truest values and beliefs, but you may not have even realized it.

These moments in life usually occur almost without any effort. They come easily and naturally because they are so aligned with our values and beliefs. They are sometimes those "ah-ha" experiences. If they come naturally, then there is nothing inside resisting them. Thus, your total self (the physical, mental, spiritual, and emotional) feels good about what you are doing. When you get this type of alignment, you usually feel happy and fulfilled. You are being true to self.

The next element of loving oneself is to feel good about oneself. I firmly believe this is all about taking good care of each of the four elements of self: the spiritual, the physical, the mental, and the emotional. How do you feel when you wake up in the morning? How do you feel when you look in the mirror?

Are you energized about life or do you take the elevator instead of the stairs whenever possible? Is your glass half-empty or half-full (or overflowing)? Let's look at each of these, although I will save the spiritual element until the next chapter.

Let's start with the physical. Now, do I think we all need to be Olympic-caliber runners with bodies like Arnold Schwarzenegger at the height of his Mr. Olympia reign? No, but I do, however, believe that we all need to be on some type of physical exercise regimen that includes proper diet, proper sleep, aerobic exercise, and anaerobic exercise. None of this has to be overwhelming. None of this has to be designed to build bulging muscles.

I have been lifting weights consistently for over 25 years and I am not even in the same galaxy as Arnold at his peak. I do, however, watch my diet, run for 20-30 minutes six days a week, and lift weights (30 to 40 minutes max) seven days a week. At the end of the day, all of this makes me feel good physically. I am never really sick and most say I have a very high energy level. All of this is related to my exercise regimen and it is one of the key enablers of my self-worth. I physically feel good and this feeds strongly into all of the other elements of me feeling good about myself. Now, I still have to see a short person when I look in the mirror in the morning, but I also remember that I have absolutely zero control over my height. But I also see someone who is in his 30's but still feels like he is in his teens. All of this has such a dramatic impact on my emotional and mental states.

There are no real excuses here. People may say things like they have to travel so much with their jobs that they cannot get on a regular exercise schedule. Well, every hotel I have stayed at in the last decade has had some type of workout facility (or, at a minimum, plenty of stairs to climb). And in those cases where I did not want to leave my room, I have easily made do with push-ups, sit-ups, and chair dips within the most elegant of hotel rooms! Don't be a victim!

As far as the mental aspects of self, we all need constant challenge and growth to our intellectual beings. The worst possible thing is to quit learning. Now, do I think we all need to be constantly enrolled in some university level class? Absolutely not, but there are many ways to constantly grow on a daily basis and exercise our mental selves without being enrolled in school.

My wife takes the time to solve that word scramble puzzle in the newspaper every day. (Recently, she has also become addicted to "Sudoku" puzzles.) Sometimes I cannot get one ounce of her attention when she gets home from work until she has completed it. Obviously she enjoys this, but it is also just a little thing each day that challenges her mentally. Reading, studying the works of great thinkers, taking a class, attending a training seminar, researching topics on the Internet...there are countless ways to exercise your mind every day. This is yet another critical step toward feeling good through exercise of the mind.

We cannot forget about the emotional. Although some of us want to maintain a "tough" exterior, we are all emotional beings. We have the need to love, to cry, to laugh, to share, to touch, and to "feel" some of these same things from others. Exercising the emotional is the toughest for me personally. I remember when my son was born. I had all of this emotion built up inside but for some reason I could not let it go at the moment. This was probably due to that tough exterior I try to maintain.

So, literally, an hour after my son was out of the womb, I told my wife I needed to go home and check on the dogs (our two dogs stay in the house and we had been gone for quite a while and they probably needed to "potty"). So, I ran to the car and started driving and just started crying my eyes out, harder than I ever cried about anything in my life. I felt so exhilarated. It was an incredible feeling. I was exercising my emotional being. And, yes, I did make it to my house in time to let the dogs relieve themselves.

Another key element for exercising emotionally focuses on giving of oneself. This includes both giving to self and giving to others. Giving to self includes all of the little things you do just for you. I mentioned earlier the mulligan I take when I go out to eat. The decadent dessert may seem like a little thing, but it is a motivator for me. It is all about giving something to me to say, "hey, thanks for running consistently all week despite the cold and rainy weather; enjoy this chocolate thunder cheesecake with raspberry sauce!" It is setting aside some quiet self time each day to read that good book or to review the newspaper. These little things can be anything and are unique to you. They are a gift to self to say "I love you." There is absolutely nothing wrong with this and is also very much needed! This is great emotional exercise. We all must ensure we invest this type of time in self.

I think you also have to give to others. This can take many forms, such as charitable giving, volunteer work, or just listening to a friend or partner. This can be anything that shows love and care for another human being. Think about anytime you have ever done these things. You inevitably feel good about yourself and it reinforces your sense of self-worth. And you love yourself for the investment you have made in another's well-being.

All of this comes back to unleashing ourselves into this world and unleashing our potential. I think we all love ourselves a little bit more when we have truly given life our all. We all really want to lie on the battlefield exhausted (and victorious, of course). A key to unleashing this potential is to truly love yourself. This love is rooted in being true to yourself. You have to find a way to discover the true you...your values, beliefs, and motivators. Once discovered, you must align all that you do with these values. This is called integrity. And you better believe that your conscience will tell you every time you do not act with integrity.

You also have to feel good about yourself spiritually, physically, mentally, and emotionally. Your physical state can have such a dominating effect on all of the other parts of self. At the same time, I am a firm believer in the criticality of balanced growth across the spiritual, mental, emotional, and physical aspects of self. As humans, we are a system, a delicate system of interrelated parts. If one component gets out of whack, it can break down the other components. When you have a cold, it tears you down mentally as much as it does physically. When you have a spat with your partner, you do not feel like doing anything physically. After a mentally draining meeting at work, you actually feel physically tired. All of these components need daily exercise and are completely within our control.

Finally, after being true to self and feeling good about ourselves, we have to give of ourselves. The recipients of this giving have to be both self and others to truly begin to love self.

So, how does this all tie back to accountability? Treating accountability as a verb is not easy. As I have mentioned, you have to be willing to take risks and not become a victim. There will be failures along the way. You will face setbacks. You will not always achieve the better outcome that you desire. You will face ridicule. The environment will try to hold you back. "They" will try to keep you down.

The only way you can successfully face all of these challenges is with a strong sense of self-worth. You must have a relentless belief in self that says it is okay to fail. Failure in one circumstance does not transform you into a failure. This sense of self-worth will actually keep you from ever experiencing a failure again. Your self-worth will start seeing these "failures" anew as simply learning experiences along your journey toward greatness. Outcomes will become less important and the focus will be on how you respond to these stimuli. Your focus will shift to those things that you control (that space between stimulus and response) and your self-worth will be measured in terms of aligning your behaviors with your values and beliefs. Self-worth will be delivered through the actions that you take every day to move toward the better that you want to become in life.

Obviously, this chapter is much easier to put into words than to put into practice. We will all face struggles and setbacks. Going it alone is difficult for all of us. Luckily, for most of us, we are never truly alone. There is a support network out there for us, but we do not always realize it or accept it. This is the focus of the next chapter.

If you think you are beaten, you are;
If you think that you dare not, you don't;
If you'd like to win and you think you can't
It's almost certain that you won't.

If you think you'll lose, you've lost;
For out in the world you'll find
Success begins with a fellow's will -
It's all in the state of mind.
If you think that you are out-classed, you are;
You've got to think high to rise;
You've got to be sure of yourself before
You can ever win a prize.
Life's battles don't always go
To the stronger or faster man;
But sooner or later, the man who wins
Is the man who thinks he can.
-Author unknown

CHAPTER NINE

You Are Not Alone

I have spent many hours over the last dozen years in conference rooms with teams of people focused on creating meaningful change. Whenever a new team comes together to attack whatever is ailing it, I like to do various ice breaker exercises to break the tension. If the team happens to be facing a "dreaded" change, I like to do a particular exercise focused on changing things about physical appearance. It is a fun exercise, yet contains a powerful set of learnings.

It involves picking a partner, studying the partner's physical appearance (clothes, jewelry, hairstyle, etc.), and then turning back to back and changing five things about your own physical appearance (such as removing your watch, taking off a sock, or parting your hair differently). The only rules are that during the change process, you cannot look at your partner and you cannot talk to your partner.

Next, the partners face each other and try to tell one another the five items the other has changed. After a few laughs, we up the ante to changing 10 *additional* items. The moans begin. Going through the same process, I announce that next we will change 15 *additional* items (we are now up to 30 total changes). After the "whining" hits an unbearable level, I tell them they do not have to change 15 additional things and everyone returns to their seats (while getting a good laugh at how funny people are looking). (Be warned! People are willing to "remove" more than you may want. For instance, I have seen way too much leg on an elderly gentleman when I did this at a chamber of commerce meeting. It is amazing how little sun an 80 year old gets...unless you live in New Mexico. Although I have never flirted with an R or PG-13 rating, I have definitely hit a solid PG!)

Finally, we debrief what they have learned. Inevitably, "real" learnings are few and far between. Remember the rules from earlier. I told them they could not look at or speak to their partners. Of course, everyone takes this to mean they cannot talk to or interact *with anyone*. Everyone thinks they are facing the challenge of this exercise alone. How much easier would this challenge have been if two or three of the folks worked together to come up with the total of 30 changes? But, instead, there is no synergy created. Individually, they struggle to find anything beyond the simple five changes. When I ask the team members if they considered using each other for this, they respond, "but you said we could not talk to our partners!" Of course, I reply, "yes, I did say you could not speak to your partner; I did not say you could not speak to anyone else!" In an instant, the team members had created a false barrier. They played this change game alone, isolated and frustrated.

The other key learning from this game if you ever want to use it involves what we lose/gain from change. Inevitably, as people change their physical appearance, things start coming off; people are losing things. Or, there is insignificant change such as a pants leg being rolled up. I hardly ever see anyone walk over to the person who took off a watch and put it on. In other words, people rarely face change from the mindset of what might I stand to gain? How often is this the way we face change within our daily lives? We focus so much on what we stand to lose that we end up losing sight of what we stand to gain. This, of course, makes us more risk averse toward change, which runs counter to aiming for the better that we desire.

How often do you live life this way? Whenever faced with a challenge or dramatic change, do you feel alone? Do you avoid exposing your challenges and burdens on others? I know that I generally do this, but I do not fully know the reasons why.

Is it because I simply do not want to burden others with my problems? Is it because of that ego inside of me that does not want to put down my defenses? For some reason, do I want to always portray a strong presence with no worries (you know, that "macho guy" inside of me)? Is it because I think the other person is not interested in helping? Is it because I simply find my strength from something else? Obviously, all of these are invalid excuses. Let's take a deeper look at each.

"I do not want to burden others" and "others are not interested in helping me." These statements may be true in your mind, but the "others" referenced in these statements do want to help you. In most cases, these others are partners, friends, parents, or other family members. Each of these groups is designed by their nature to lend a helping hand in the form of advice, relevant experience, a shoulder to cry on, or just a listening ear. All of these groups are designed to love you unconditionally. And if you do not give them the opportunity to love you, you are depriving them of doing something they long to do. You are actually not showing them the love they deserve to trust them to want to sincerely help you. Love from family and friendship is one the greatest gifts in the world, but you have to be willing to accept it.

If these two statements were actually true ("I do not want to burden others" and "others are not interested in helping me), then I would question the motives of the so-called friends and family members. In almost all cases, however, both of these groups will want to sincerely help you through whatever challenges and changes you are facing. Individually, we have to be willing to provide full disclosure and be open to the help these "others" long to provide. By allowing this love into your life, your ability to "let go" and face your challenges and changes head-on will grow exponentially through your newfound collective strength.

All of this begins by creating and nurturing meaningful relationships with family and friends. Open communication, sincere care, and understanding one another are all at the heart of these meaningful relationships. All of this translates into trust. If you are not willing to trust me enough to disclose your needs, this ends up speaking volumes about how much you actually care about me. In turn, our relationship regresses.

So, if you want to create meaningful change within your own life and take full accountability for it, you need to invest time every day building more meaningful relationships with your partner, family, and friends. This investment will translate into greater inner strength when you need it most...when you face the challenge of change within your own life. I am reminded of some of the lines from "Friends" by Michael W. Smith, which equally apply to family and friends:

"Friends are friends forever...friends will not say never, because the welcome will not end...because a lifetime is not too long to live as friends."

These words are so true! It is up to you to gain the most you can out of the opportunity of family and friendship. Give to these the most you can and take from them the most you can. Strength should come from both directions of giving and receiving.

How often do you demonstrate behaviors that reflect "that ego inside of me that does not want to put down my defenses" or "for some reason, I want to always portray a strong presence with no worries and be a macho man?" Too many of us have way too much self-pride. Even around those we are closest to, we want to portray this image of strength. Nobody wants to come across as weak. Have you ever been in a class where the teacher is speaking another language and when she asks if anyone has any questions, not a soul raises their hand? You look around, knowing that you are in the same state of confusion as everyone else, but you are not willing to be the first "dummy" to ask a question. Why do we behave this way? The smart person may know the answers, but the effective one asks the question. And all of this is about being effective! There are no stupid questions, as the old saying goes, only stupid people not willing to ask them. But, our pride and ego get in the way. We would rather fail than show weakness in public. We could all use a very large dose of vulnerability.

Vulnerability is so critical when it comes to seeking help. We all need to have a willingness to say I cannot survive, much less thrive, if I go it alone. As we have mentioned before, vulnerability is all about exposing everything about self with no shame. It is about saying "this is me; I am not perfect, but I want better; will you help?" And I am willing to bet that all parts of your support network (partner, other family, friends, etc.) are more than willing to do whatever it takes to help you.

It all starts with your willingness to let go of your pride and defenses. Your ego has to take a backseat to the better you are longing for in life. Otherwise, you will continue to have to go it alone. And in the end you will not get as far as you would like, especially compared to how far you would have gotten through the strength of your support network.

Vulnerability is the key to this. Defined as a willingness to expose oneself to physical or emotional injury, when showing vulnerability to family or friends, you do not have to worry about these repercussions. As mentioned before, if you do have to worry about these things, then I would question the motives of these so-called family and friends. Once again, the key to this is constantly building and nurturing meaningful relationships with the members of your support network.

Now, I fully realize that there are some of us who truly live alone. I cannot claim to fully understand what this is like. I have always been blessed with a strong and loving family and many wonderful friends. I have an incredible partner in Betsy who is always there for me. If you are in this situation of "living on an island," I can only offer one piece of advice, which ties back to my original question in this chapter:

How often do I live life this way? Whenever faced with a challenge or dramatic change, do I feel alone? Do I avoid exposing my challenges and burdens on others? I know that I generally do this, but do not fully know the reasons why.

I know that, in general, I do not burden family or friends with my "problems." If I play back in my mind the last 100 dialogues I have had with family, friends, or co-workers, 99 of them have focused on the needs of the other. Is this because I am just that unselfish? Absolutely not! Is it because I do not believe my family or friends want to be burdened with my problems? Definitely not! Is this because of my ego and desire to appear strong? It could be, but at least not at the current depths of my thinking.

The answer actually lies in the only answer I have for those who are "living on an island." I believe my strength comes from my personal relationship with Jesus Christ. Now, I do not want this to become a sermon by any means, but I do want to offer my personal testimony. And I would offer to those living on that island in isolation that God is a support resource who is always there for all of us and with absolutely no discrimination based on pedigree, degree, or any other status. All God wants is an open heart and a desire for change. God wants vulnerability and faith that He will see us through our most difficult times.

I was raised going to church from birth. Prayer has always been something I have known and, more importantly, trusted. Deriving strength from this faith is one of those difficult things to explain. I have never seen the burning bush nor has a lake parted for me to cross. I have never touched the hole in Jesus' pierced hands nor had 10 hamburgers feed 5000 people. But I do believe I hear the voice of God literally every day of my life. And this voice provides me with strength and comfort.

This might just be a false belief on my part, but I believe that the voice inside of my heart and head that talks to me all of the time is the voice of God. Yes, some will call this my conscience. I call it my coach who is constantly providing me with feedback and advice to navigate through the many challenges of life. And it is incredibly comforting to have that voice. It is inner strength. And through that inner strength I can live without fear. I absolutely know that God is with me. Does this mean that everything goes my way? Absolutely not, as I am still human and will make many, many mistakes. God is, however, there to pick me up and help me figure out how to make fewer mistakes the next time. He helps (or tries real hard) to keep me aligned with my true self (my vision).

It is through this relationship with God that I have strength to take risks, to show vulnerability, and, in reality, to have opportunities instead of problems. Do I struggle with this? Of course I do. But at the end of the day when I have a concern or problem, I pray about it. And then I go to sleep. While others will toss and turn all night, I have an inner peace to trust that God will see me through it. Some might view this as naïve, but I just view it as faith.

Once again, I am not here to say that my religious beliefs are right and yours are not. I am here to say, though, that my personal relationship with Jesus Christ is my own ultimate source of strength in facing the many challenges of change within my life. This spiritual strength can take other forms in your own life based on your own beliefs. But I do firmly believe that we are fooling ourselves if we believe there is not a greater being out there who wants to be (and should be) our ultimate source of strength. This type of faith takes the strongest type of vulnerability. It is believing without seeing. But at the end of the day, if you want to get the most out of life and take the highest degree of accountability, you are going to need more strength than most of us can possibly sustain as humans. There has to be a "higher power" source for this strength. I would challenge that your spiritual self is the only possible source for this ultimate strength.

Personal success, happiness, and fulfillment all require us to accept full accountability for self. This is incredibly challenging and difficult; it is that much more so if faced alone. Most all of us have an incredible support network of friends and family wanting and waiting to be a source of strength for us. The question is "are you willing to show some vulnerability and accept this special gift of love?" To maximize this source of strength, we all need to invest time on a daily basis in building and nurturing meaningful relationships with the members of our support network.

We all have the opportunity to gain ultimate strength through our spiritual growth stemming from faith in a higher power. I fully accept that this higher power can take different forms based on our individual beliefs. Mine comes through my personal relationship with Jesus Christ. From this, I gain incredible strength and peace. And this comes even though I am probably only about one-tenth of the Christian I should be. I can only imagine the peace and strength I would feel if I were as faithful as God wants me to be. But at the end of the day, I know that I feel comfort and strength inside to face any challenge every day of my life simply through the power of prayer. Does this guarantee "victory?" Absolutely not; but remember, we need to learn to not measure success by outcomes, but by personal effectiveness, which focuses only on the things we have complete control over.

If this is something you struggle with, there are plenty of resources out there willing to help. Just find a church, synagogue, or other temple of faith and go. It might take some exploring to find the religion that is true to your beliefs. But the important thing is to make the effort, follow through, and be faithful to the true beliefs that you discover. Who cares if you end up Baptist, Catholic, Muslim, or Mormon? The important thing is to find your spiritual self and nurture it. Exercise it daily just as we discussed earlier with your physical self. This will ultimately become your greatest source of strength...to know that you are truly not living your life and facing its many challenges alone. And treating accountability as a verb in your life will become that much easier.

Footprints in the Sand

One night I dreamed I was walking along the beach with the Lord.
Many scenes from my life flashed across the sky.
In each scene I noticed footprints in the sand.
Sometimes there were two sets of footprints,
other times there were one set of footprints.

This bothered me because I noticed
that during the low periods of my life,
when I was suffering from
anguish, sorrow or defeat,
I could see only one set of footprints.

ACCOUNTABILITY...A NOUN OR A VERB?

So I said to the Lord,
"You promised me, Lord,
that if I followed you,
you would walk with me always.
But I have noticed that during the most trying periods of my life
there have only been one set of footprints in the sand.
Why, when I needed you most, have you not been there for me?"

The Lord replied,
"The times when you have seen only one set of footprints in the sand,
is when I carried you."

-Mary Stevenson

CHAPTER TEN

You Are Only Accountable For You

You have no choice but to be accountable for you. The choice you do have is whether or not to treat accountability as a verb in your life. Regardless, when thinking about accountability for the better that you desire, the buck stops with you.

The buck also stops with you in terms of who you are accountable for, although we each behave sometimes as though we are accountable for many more people beyond ourselves. We are all much too quick to place the critical eye upon others as though we were accountable for their behaviors and actions. We are all too well-quipped to know what is best for others...or so we think.

Now, I do accept that at times in our lives we are accountable for others. When my son was born, Betsy and I were fully accountable for his life and all of his needs, as an infant is completely dependent. But over time, even at a young age, people naturally begin moving toward an independent stage. And if we want our child to grow and succeed in discovering self, we will let this occur. Betsy and I will allow our son to share accountability and, ultimately, move toward a full passing of accountability to him for his own well-being. Obviously, the maturation of our child and the trust built in our relationship determines the rate in which this transition occurs. But it must occur.

At the other end of the spectrum, many of us have aging parents who are losing their independence because of various physical or mental limitations. I also accept that some account-ability over others can occur here as well.

But in general, beyond young children, aging parents, or other people with special needs (various handicaps, etc.), we need to let go of our desire to act accountably for others. Not doing this will ultimately put a strain on the relationship or keep the other individual from taking on the accountability he/she needs for growth. Regardless of how well-intentioned you might be, you are ultimately hurting that person by taking away some of his/her accountability. Worse yet, by straining the relationship, you could be reducing some of the strength you may need from your support network during those challenging times.

Beyond the situations above, where we should take or share accountability for others, why are we so quick to act as though we are accountable for others' well-being? Why do we think we know what is best for others? With no proof at all, I think that we sometimes act out in others what we want for ourselves. The criticality we are placing on others is really criticality we have of ourselves.

So why place this on others? I think the answer lies within the various chapters of this book. By placing the burden of our own accountabilities on others, we do not have to take the risk on ourselves. How many of us try to drive our children down the paths that we were afraid to take earlier in our lives? By placing it on others, we do not have to face the failure. We do not have to have a strong sense of self-worth if it is someone else who is taking the risk. We can avoid the buck stopping with us.

It is so much easier to hold the mirror up to someone else and so hard to hold it up to ourselves. If we hold it up to ourselves, we have to see all of the "stains" and ugliness within each of us and yet still believe we can succeed. In other words, acting accountably for someone else is easy because we are never truly accountable. Why waste this precious time and energy when it could be used to take action in our own lives?

Now, I firmly believe in caring for others and offering needed coaching and counseling (or just listening) to help them succeed. But there is a big difference between *telling* people what they should do versus *helping them discover* what they should do. The former creates walls and the latter creates bridges. And bridges nurture your relationships and strengthen your support network. A stronger support network will only enable you to be that much more effective with your own accountability.

At the end of the day, you want to always do all that you can to nurture relationships, build the strength of your support network, and maximize your ability to act accountably. Being accountable for self and following the principles outlined in this book will accomplish these things. Trying to act accountable for others will break them down. Obviously, you are accountable for the choice you make in these situations. But try to think "bridges" versus "walls."

"Some of us have great runways already built for us. If you have one, take OFF! But if you don't have one, realize it is your responsibility to grab a shovel and build one for yourself and for those who will follow after you." -Amelia Earhart

CHAPTER ELEVEN

Ending At The Beginning

"God, grant me the serenity to accept the outcomes I experience in life and help me to use them to learn and grow wiser; give me the courage to use that space between stimulus and response to create the better that I desire in my life and the vulnerability to treat accountability as a verb!"

We all want better in our lives. Happiness and fulfillment are not entitlements, though; they are the by-products we experience from taking action in our lives that is aimed toward this better we want. True happiness and fulfillment do not come cheap in terms of effort, persistence, and time. This should be viewed as a journey, for if treated as a destination, you are selling yourself short. The better that you want out of your life should be constantly rising. This, of course, is totally up to you. But I believe if you truly look deep within yourself, you will always want better. Choosing fulfillment over contentment should be an easy choice. Putting this into practice is a different story.

We are all accountable for this better that we desire whether we like it or not. By default, accountability sits squarely on your shoulders for your life and everything about you. This is accountability the noun. No action required. As defined, this form of accountability simply means the buck stops with you.

You have no choice about this. If you are driving the car and get pulled over for speeding, you are accountable. There are no excuses. You are accountable for every decision you ever make. But does this form of accountability really make you stronger, helping you thrive toward the better that you desire? My answer is no.

Accepting accountability is the key foundational first step toward achieving the better that you desire, but ONLY if you treat it as a verb in your life. Treating anything as a verb means translating it into action. Only through action will you achieve better. This can be better father, child, student, soccer player, nurse, or friend. It takes the form of any better that you desire. If you are truly accountable for better at any of these roles you play or for the experiences you have in life, you will take action. If there is no action, I say wholeheartedly that you are not truly accountable. And, if you think you are truly accountable, I question whether or not you really want better. You have to treat accountability as a verb in your life if you want better and this means taking action.

Every day, we are blessed with a tiny space between stimulus and response. We own this space. We are fully accountable (as a noun) for this space and no action is required. It is in this space where we make every decision we ever make, decide all of the actions we are going to take, and put our behaviors into motion. It is in this space that our current and future character takes shape. It is in this space where we decide to be stagnant, regress, or progress. Obviously, if we are aiming for better, we want progress.

Progress only comes from action. Thus, we are only accepting accountability if we are willing to use that space between stimulus and response to take action toward the better that we want out of life. Accountability as a verb is a requirement for this desired progress. Walking the walk is required.

You have already learned in this book of the many heroes in this world who used this space between stimulus and response to achieve better. They used this space to demonstrate their true accountability. Viktor Frankl will always be the most vivid example of this for me. Under the most extreme and challenging of circumstances, he did not lose sight of his accountability for that space between stimulus and response. He used this space to overcome death and emotional destruction. Lacey Heward used this space to overcome an incredible physical handicap to become a world-class athlete. The 1980 U.S. Olympic Hockey Team used this space to execute one the biggest (if not *the* biggest) upset victories in the history of sport when they defeated the highly trained and widely favored Russian team. "Jason" used this space to do normal things such as coon hunting despite his blindness; he did not use this space to be a victim. None of these examples treated accountability as a noun. These people used this space to take action, treat accountability as a verb, and achieve true greatness. Is this not the better that we all want?

The inner peace we can all feel about this is the fact that no special degrees, pedigrees, or other physical attributes are required. Humans of any sex, race, creed, color, age, or origin have equal opportunity to use this space between stimulus and response to achieve any better they desire. This space does not discriminate on any dimension other than the willingness to truly accept accountability. It is really completely up to you. But you cannot just want it. You must take action by treating accountability as a verb!

It all starts with having a willingness to take the risk. Your desire for the better has to be greater than your fear of losing. Unfortunately, the better that we want can never come without some form of risk. We cannot allow ourselves to be fooled into thinking that by not going for better we are eliminating the risk. In reality, there is just as much risk associated with settling for stagnation as there is in aiming for fulfillment. None of this is easy, but it is the price that you have to be willing to pay in order to achieve the better that you want.

Once you have decided to take the risk, you then need to be grounded in reality. You must have a firm grasp regarding what you can and cannot control. And this requires a paradigm shift if you want to be successful. Society teaches us to focus on outcomes and to control our destinies. In reality, the only thing we can control in this life is the responses that we provide in that space between stimulus and response. Thus, the only thing we can control is our behaviors. We must unlearn what society has taught us and not worry about outcomes. Our focus should be on our behaviors. And if we aim our behaviors in the right direction (with our full energy and persistency), the outcomes we desire will usually fall into place. The paradigm shift is the belief that we will get better outcomes in our lives by not focusing on outcomes.

Throughout this growth process, we have to avoid becoming a victim. This mentality usually stands out in our language ("Woe is me," "I deserve...," "I can't believe they did that to me," "They need to do something different,") but, unfortunately, manifests itself in our behaviors. We start focusing on changing others instead of changing ourselves. Or, worse, we choose not to act because of the false belief of "what's the use, I will fail anyway." Oh God, forgive me when I whine. You have blessed me with that tiny space between stimulus and response, the world is mine!

The journey to better is not an easy one and it would be quite impossible to achieve better without a road map. We all need a vision of the person we are aiming to be. This does not need to be the perfectly worded paragraph worthy of the printed page. It just needs to be true to you, reflective of your values and beliefs. Think about those times in life when you felt best about what you were doing, when you felt natural and completely at ease. It is moments like these that most likely reflect the true you.

You have to have a strong belief in self. This is not cockiness or false belief in self. This is self-confidence with a strong sense of humility. This is all about strong self-awareness balanced with an inner vulnerability to be true to your strengths and weaknesses. There will be many pitfalls and stumbling blocks along the way. It is this belief in self that will enable you to get going in the first place and keep you on track when you fall down. Remember, "God does not make any crap!" We all have self-worth.

This required feeling of self-worth necessitates a daily focus on physical, mental, emotional, and spiritual growth. All four of these components of self require daily exercise. And it is the little things and focusing on them that make the difference, like taking the stairs instead of the elevator or drinking water at meals instead of a soda or eliminating butter from your diet or waking up 30 minutes earlier each morning to read a devotion or setting aside 15 minutes each day for completely uninter-rupted and unconditional listening for your partner. The list of little things you can do daily to grow across these four dimen-sions is limitless. And before long, the list of little things creates huge results.

The hardest thing you can do is face all of this alone. Few of us are truly alone and all of us have the opportunity to find and nurture our spiritual selves to ensure that we are never alone. Support beyond self can take many forms every day, including family, friends, co-workers, teachers, ministers, and spiritual be-ings. All of these make up your support network and provide you with the strength (and in many cases knowledge) that you will need to stay on this journey and succeed. It is critical to nurture strong and meaningful relationships with the members of your support network. And strength will come from both your giving and receiving within this network.

It all comes back to that space between stimulus and re-sponse and how you use it. You own it regardless, but will you use it to take action? This action should reflect your strongest desire to take ownership of your life and the better that you want. It should reflect a vision for self that is true to your val-ues and beliefs. This action should promote growth across your physical, mental, emotional, and spiritual selves.

It is in this space where you will refuse to be a victim. You are in control, full of energy and zeal. Your belief in self will lead you to take the risk necessary to achieve the better that you desire. And in the end, you will accomplish the outcomes that you wanted in the beginning by not focusing on them.

It is my wish that you will just go for it. You will go for it with no fear of repercussion or failure. Starting right now, you will aim for fulfillment over contentment. Regardless, you are accountable as we have already discussed (the noun). The challenge now is to redefine yourself by redefining accountability as a verb within your life. Hold that mirror up to your face and ask yourself, "What better do I desire? What actions can I take today to move toward that better?"

You have taken your first action (and, thus, treated accountability as a verb) by completing this book. What will be your next action?

"Today is the Very First Day of the Rest of My Life."
This is the Beginning of a New Day.
I Can Waste It ... or Use It For Good.
But What I Do Today is Important,
Because I am Exchanging a Day of My Life For It.
When Tomorrow Comes, This Day Will Be Gone Forever,
Leaving in Its Place Something That I Have Traded For It.
I Want It to Be Gain and Not Loss, Good and Not Evil,
Success and Not Failure, in Order That I Not Regret the Price I Have Paid For It.
I Will Give 100% of Myself Just For Today, For You Never Fail

Until You Stop Trying.
I Will Be the Kind of Person I have Always Wanted
To Be...
I Have Been Given This Day to Use as I Will
-Author Unknown.

"A love like no other"
by Manju
Peace, tranquility, fulfillment
All around spring flourishes
Endless beauty, comfort, security.

Bliss, fulfillment, contentment.
Emotions high, feelings soar,
Joy overflows, hopes realized
Souls entwine, hearts unite
Bodies become one.

I do not know if "dedication" is the most appropriate word, but it seems to be the word most authors use for this part of their books. The more appropriate word for me might be inspiration.

My inspiration is my soul mate, my best friend, my workout partner, and my lover. Lucky for me, all of these represent one person...Betsy, my wife. Words cannot describe the inspiration I receive from her every day. She is the inspiration I have to achieve better every day in all aspects of my life.

Betsy is my inspiration to treat accountability as a verb in my life. I want to be "better" every day not only for me, but more so for her. This includes better husband, better father, and better growth in my physical, spiritual, mental, and emotional selves. I want her to always be proud of me in all that I do. Thus, given the inspiration she gives me and how it ties to the focus of this book, I dedicate it to her and commit to trying harder and harder every day to live by its principles.

Betsy makes me want to treat love as a verb. I want to take more and more action every day to demonstrate my love for her. I want to do all of the little things I can do every day for her to feel my love (remember the "3 C's" of coffee, clothes, and chocolate?). She is the queen of my life and I want my actions to reflect this. I hate to steal a line from Jerry Maguire, but Betsy truly "completes me."

Ironically, when I met Betsy, I was not looking for love. What I found out is that you cannot really look for love. True love finds you. And it is not one of those things that you can analyze and "figure out." You just know it and feel it in your heart. And, by gosh, it makes you feel incredible all over. I feel sorry for those who have never experienced true love. There can be no greater high in this world.

I stated earlier that my vision was to live to be 100 years old. Most of this is motivated by my desire to love Betsy for as long as I can in this lifetime. Every day is a new experience with her and represents a deepening of my unconditional love for her. I look forward to growing old with her.

This is my dedication. She is my inspiration. She is my soul mate. She is my best friend. She is my workout partner. She is my lover.

She is Betsy.

More than anything else I can think of, having a victim mentality will keep you from succeeding. It will suck the life right out of your will to improve. It will create this false belief that you have no say in the outcomes in your life. Remember, success should not be tied directly to outcomes but to how you respond to the circumstances you face in life. Your behaviors and your responses are all that you control and, thus, the true measure of your character and success in life.

ABOUT THE AUTHOR

Richard Cassidy graduated from Clemson University and earned his MBA from the Kenan-Flagler Business School of UNC-Chapel Hill. A career counselor and corporate consultant, the author resides with his wife and son in Hillsborough, NC.